THE NINJA SWORD
ART OF SILENT KENJUTSU

THE NINJA SWORD

ART OF SILENT KENJUTSU

by

Katsumi Toda

Published by

dragon books

Acknowledgements

Publisher	David Chambers
Editor	Lesley Anne Copp-Taylor
Line drawings & photography	Malcolm Copp-Taylor
Layout & Design	Island Design

U.S. Distributor
Sakura Dragon Corporation
Thousand Oaks, California

Printed by Anchor Brendon Ltd
Tiptree, Essex, United Kingdom
First Published April 1986

ISBN 0 946062 15 3
L.C.C.C. No. 86-70371

"For years I forged my spirit through
the study of swordsmanship,
Confronting all challenges resolutely.
The walls surrounding suddenly breaking down;
As clear dewdrops reflect the world clearly,
Satori comes!"

After YAMAOKA TESSHU (1836-1888)
Swordsman, Politician, Artist, Zen Master.

Contents

To all my Friends.

It pleases me greatly to know that you enjoy the works that I have offered so far.

In response to your many letters and cards; from all parts of the world, I am surprised sometimes to receive notification from my publishers, that another person has enjoyed my work sufficiently to write. There are not enough hours in the day for me to reply personally to you all. I trust that this "Open" letter will suffice; I am most gratified that my message is appreciated by such a diverse audience.

Following the amazing success of "The Ninja Star . . . Art of Shuriken-Jutsu", I have been asked by my publishers, Dragon Books, to write something concerning what I would best describe as "Silent Ken-Jutsu". To fully do justice to this immense task, would in my estimation involve several volumes, and possibly thirty plus years in the writing; I trust that one day this will become a reality. For the immediate moment however, I trust that this work will at least "provoke some comment". However, as with all things the opinions expressed are of a personal nature. I welcome constructive criticism, for that is how we truly progress.

I would say one thing in parting, and that is, "For every action there is a truth, and for every truth there is an action". Let us strive to have the honesty to make such an action, that we may create a truth.

To the many unknown friends
I offer a heartfelt welcome.
I remain, yours sincerely

TODA KATSUMI.

DISCLAIMER

The techniques and Arts described in this book are capable of killing. That is the very nature of the Arts as they were formulated in the past. This book is not purporting to be a manual of killing techniques, far from it, it is a sociological study of an aspect of a feudal culture and the networks of control within that society.

Neither the publishers nor the author will be held responsible for any physical injury, or damage of any sort, that may occur as a result of reading and/or following the instructions given herein. It is essential therefore, that before attempting any of the physical activities described or depicted in this book, the reader or readers should consult a qualified physician to ascertain whether the reader or readers should engage in the physical activity described or depicted in this book.

As the physical activities described or depicted herein may be overly taxing or sophisticated for the reader or readers, it is essential that this advice be followed and a physician consulted.

Simplified map of feudal Japan showing
approximate positions of the "Godaken"
five traditions of sword making.

BIZEN

YAMASHIRO

MINO

YAMATO

SAGAMI

Kana for the five traditions

山城
YAMASHIRO

備前
BIZEN

相模
SAGAMI

美濃
MINO

大和
YAMATO

1. HISTORICAL BACKGROUND

Let me say, first and foremost, that the Ninja Sword was not necessarily a straight edged short sword, as popularized by the media, and persons who have not researched the subject well enough. The shape of the blade used by the feudal Ninja could be the form of any of the major derivative sword styles.

These are notably, and traditionally known as the GOKADEN, literally the five traditions. They take their name from their origination in one of the feudal provinces of Old Japan (i.e. pre Meiji −1868 period). The names are as follows:−

YAMASHIRO

SAGAMI (AKA SOSHU)

BIZEN

MINO

YAMATO

To be precise, we refer to these by the separate title of DEN, thus each of the five traditions would be, Yamashiro-Den, Sagami-Den (AKA Soshu-Den), Bizen-Den, Mino-Den, and Yamato-Den. This is of course to place them firmly in the "Golden Age" of Ninjutsu, which most scholars agree was the period roughly speaking over eight hundred years ago, with the bloody wars of the Gempei. Of this I will speak no further, merely advising the reader to refer to chapters one, two and three of the companion volume to this . . . . "The Ninja Star − Art of Shuriken Jutsu", published by Dragon Books. It is wasteful repetition to go over already trodden ground. Let us continue; in the traditional, purist sense, the Gokaden is seen as the first flower of the Koto Period (literally "Old Sword" period) it was really the work of the notable swordsmiths of that time, whose experiments produced blades of unsurpassed quality and sharpness. Sadly many of these secrets were lost in the turbulent years of war, before the great TOSHOGU (Tokugawa Iyeyasu) unified Japan in the early 1600's. It is pleasing to note that there are several swordsmiths working at the time of writing this book; who are striving to rediscover the secrets of the gokaden. I pause here to mention one such swordsmith, who has been most helpful to me in my researches, he is Tō-shō Kobayashi (Kobayashi Yasuhiro), whom many of you will recognise as being the maker of the fine sword blades used in my friend Mr. Obata's book upon the subject of 'tameshigiri'.

To return to the subject;.the major smiths of the gokaden can be ascribed as follows:–

Sanjo Munechika of Yamashiro
Masamune of Sagami (Soshu)
Tomonari of Bizen
Kaneuji of Mino
Amakuni of Yamato

I apologise to those of you who have not had their favourite smith mentioned in my very simplified list, but I must assume that not all of us are as my English friends would say "Sword Buffs" *(One who is an avid student of the Classical Japanese Sword . . . Ed)*. So in this general way, let us go on. We must set firmly the precise historical background to the development of the Japanese sword, both in its shape and its spirit, for without understanding this, we may fall into the morass of half heard legend. This is of course especially true when we are confronted by the phenomenon of Ninja. Now let me say first and foremost, that I do not profess to have any great knowledge, practical or otherwise, of the modern expression of the feudal Ninja, and so bearing this in mind, I shall confine my comments in the main to the feudal, some may say traditional ninja arts. Having said this, I am at pains to stress that I am in no way denigrating the fine efforts of the modern experimenters and pioneers of what may in future years be known as the "Renaissance of Ninjutsu". Without their sterling efforts much of the genki (Vigour) of the Ninja arts would be lost in the dust of crumbling Emaki scrolls. Let us open and read those secrets with a light heart, and learn that the heart of darkness was indeed a flower to be nurtured. Thus the shapes, and their names were:–

Tsurugi or Ken
Tachi
Handachi
Katana
Wakizashi
Tanto

In very simple terms, the major sword shapes can be described as . . . .

TSURUGI OR KEN This, researchers are fairly sure is the first "Nippon-To". It was a straight double edged sword with a sharpened point, it mainly existed as a relevant weapon in the period between the seventh to ninth centuries. It is generally recognised as being the form that the deity Fudo myo-o carries with him in his many appearances on items of art work; such as swords and in inspirational paintings.

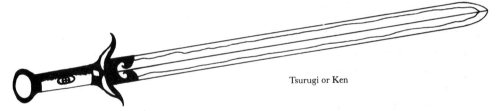

Tsurugi or Ken

TACHI Strictly speaking, a tachi is a slung sword, usually held by two rings or chain mail fastenings, this was tied at the waist of a warrior, and worn edge downwards. This was particularly useful when riding, and its use is mainly in the years of the vast cavalry engagements of the tenth century onwards.

Tachi in Heian Court Style

3

HANDACHI, in shape, though not necessarily in age, is a rough transition between the Tachi and Katana forms, or more reasonably between the "Jindachi Zukuri" form and the "Buke Zukuri" form. To some traditionalists, the Jindachi Zukuri form is far the most elegant, it is worthwhile to note; the "Shin-Gunto" (Military Sword from the Second World War period) was modelled upon the Jindachi Zukuri form.

Handachi

KATANA This is the typical so called "Samurai" sword, it is usually no longer than thirty six inches (90cms) and no less than twenty three inches (60cms). It came into use during the Muromachi Period, which was about 1392-1572. The curved blade is worn edge uppermost, thrust through the 'obi' (a wide belt wrapped many times around the waist).

Katana

WAKIZASHI Traditionally this was the shorter companion to the katana. When worn by a Samurai, it was known as Dai-Sho, literally "big-little", it became the very badge of office in feudal Japan, no one who was not of Samurai status was allowed, on pain of death to even attempt to wear Dai-Sho. Some classes, such as merchants or doctors were permitted to wear wakizashi. There is in the collection of a good friend of mine, a long sword mounting, which to all intents and purposes looks to be a katana, but upon drawing the blade, it reveals itself to be a short wakizashi. My first impression was that it was a blade that had been placed in a long scabbard, but its owner pointed out to me that all the fittings were, as they say in the antique world, "en suite".

That is to say, they were matching, so the possibility of the shorter blade being placed in the longer saya (scabbard) was remote. My friend then let me know the secret of his treasure, it was owned by a rich Osaka merchant in the last quarter of the eighteenth century. Since that time I have seen many such examples, I suppose one could refer to this as a "sheep in wolf's clothing" to paraphrase your saying. Clearly in this example the rich merchant wished to impress that he was Samurai, whilst protecting himself from prosecution . . . . ah! such is life.

Wakizashi

TANTO Basically anything shorter than wakizashi may be referred to as tanto, but exactly what wakizashi length is, is certainly open to much academic discussion. I am of the opinion that anything less than twelve inches blade length is tanto. I must now further break down tanto into its sub-divisions. With a guard, we may call it 'handachi' without; then we refer to it as 'aikuchi' (literally "meeting mouth"). If we have an exceptionally thick blade, we may refer to it as "yoroi-doshi" (armour piercer). Women wore a small dagger, with which to protect their honour, this is referred to as 'kai ken'.

There is a rare form of scabbarded truncheon, which externally looks like a large tanto, this has come to be known as "kabuto-wari" which is freely translated as "helmet smasher". They are fairly rare items, and I doubt that they ever were seriously used in time of war, I am afraid I would date that item firmly in the mid-seventeenth, early eighteenth century, which was relatively peaceful under the control of the Bakufu Government of the Tokugawa Shoguns.

Tanto

Kabuto-Wari

So we have discussed the major traditions, and the main styles of edged weapons; let us now pay particlar attention to the shape of the Japanese Sword.

Shapes of the blade can be simplified as the following:—

KOSHIZORI
TORIIZORI
SAKIZORI
UCHIZORI
MUZORI

KOSHIZORI is the classical "old" style with the curve centre near to the tang end, or even in the tang itself.

Koshizori

TORIIZORI, like the shape of the torii arch, has its centre of curvature approximately in the centre of the blade.

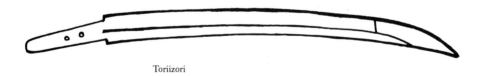

Toriizori

SAKIZORI, which can be likened to the mirror image of the koshizori, has its centre of curvature nearer to the point end of the blade.

Sakizori

UCHIZORI This is really the area of tanto, but to be brief its curvature is slightly towards the edge.

Uchizori

MUZORI This is the classic "Ninja" sword shape in the common opinion, it is however not the sole preserve of the Ninja. It was the earliest of single edged blades, and in later years became the preserve of the "shikomi-zue" or "sword cane" of the late nineteenth century. However to assume that a shikomi-zue mounted cane is of Ninja origin is to misinterpret utterly that which is at heart the late nineteenth century passion for intricate and "tricky" items, but more of that later.

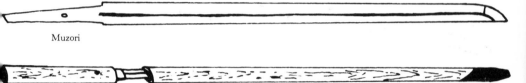

Muzori

Shikomi-Zue

Having discussed, albeit in simple terms the shapes in which blades were made, we must also be aware of the blade's shape, as it were in cross section. Thus we have the types known as:—

KIRIHA-ZUKURI
HIRA-ZUZURI
SHINOGI-ZUKURI
KISSAKI-MOROHA-ZUKURI

KIRIHA-ZUKURI seen in cross section has flat sides, with a meeting point of the two angles at the blade edge.

Kiriha Zukuri

HIRA-ZUKURI is a simple triangle form, seen in cross section, it has no appreciable ridge line.

Hira-Zukuri

SHINOGI-ZUKURI is the classic, and most widespread form of manufacture, it is fair to say that the ridge line narrows to the back of the blade, to which it is closer than the deeper angle to the edge.

Shinogi-Zukuri

KISSAKI-MOROHA-ZUKURI usually ascribed to Amakuni, whose name appears under the Yamato Tradition. This style is usually described as "Little Crow" or Kogarasu-Maru-Zukuri, it is double-edged near the point, similar to some Western bayonets of the nineteenth century, though the style predates them by some seven centuries. It runs single-edged to the hilt on the other side, with a lengthwise ridge running down the centre of the blade.

Kissaki-Moroha-Zukuri

With this form, we must also take into account, in the historical development, the shape of the back of the blade, and also the tang shape. In the main they are of the three main types as follows:—

IORIMUNE
MARUMUNE
MITSUMUNE

Simply, this is . . . . **Iorimune** refers to a ridged back, like a roof of a house.

Marumune refers to a crown rounded back, like half a circle.

Mitsumune, as its name implies is a three sided shape of back, I have heard it referred to as "ridge tile" shape, though the standard "three sided" will suffice.

Iorimune

Maramune

Mitsuhune

Now looking at the shape of the tang, which some scholars believe is more telling than a signature, it is generally accepted that the shape of the tang denotes the school, but as I advised in my work on Shuriken . . . . "Watch out! you could get caught". There is deceit and trickery everwhere, some of it intended, so be careful, but it is safe to generalise upon the following:–

KIJI-MOMO
FUNAGATA
FURI-SODE
TANAGO-BARA
KURI-JIRI (HIRA-YAMAGATA-)
HA-AGARI KURI-JIRI
KATA-YAMAGATA
KENGYO
KIRI-ICHI-MONJI

KIJI-MOMO is rather charmingly referred to as "pheasant thigh", due to its bevelled-in shape. There are those who say that it was not used after the mid thirteen hundreds.

Kiji-Momo

FUNAGATA this is known as the 'ship's keel', or sometimes the 'ship's bottom', due to its obvious similarity to the keel of the ship.

Funa-Gata

FURISODE due to its curved shape, this has been called the "kimono sleeve".

Furi-Sode

TANAGO-BARA referred to as fish stomach, or somewhat humourously as "fish belly" due to its similarity with the underside of a carp. It was the favourite shape of the notorious Muramasa of Ise. It was he, who was considered to be the "mad swordsmith", in fact his madness was said to be transferred into his blades; which have a reputation for blood-thirsty behaviour in its owners. Tokugawa Ieyasu disliked them considerably, having reputedly cut himself whilst looking at a friend's Muramasa blade. There is a further tale, which says that Ieyasu tried to commit seppuku (Ritual Suicide) but the blade would not cut; dropping the blade he went on to win the battle which he thought had been lost. After the fray he noticed that the blade that he had tried to kill himself with, was one made by Muramasa, though there are those who believe it must have been a fake as no true Muramasa blade could resist tasting blood. Well whatever the case, the tanago-bara is certainly a popular shape.

Tanago-Bara

KURI-JIRI (Hira-Yamagata), chestnut shaped is all that really comes to mind with this form, that and the fact that it is probably the most used of tang shapes.

Kuri-Jiri

HA-AGARI KURI-JIRI I always think that this form looks like the back of the Daibutsu (great bronze statue of Buddha) in Kamakura. I know that the master founder Tanji Hisatomo was reputed to have links with swordsmiths, but I think that this is far too tenuous an explanation to be of any merit. I include it more as an item of interest than of actual fact. Be that as it may, the shape with its back edge curvature is most refined in its form.

KATA-YAMAGATA This is the shoulder single bevel, cutting at an angle. It always reminds me of the Katakana symbol – 'he', which as you know are the Japanese phonetic symbols for spelling non-Japanese names, such as photograph or micro-chip.

Kata-Yamagata

KENGYO this is simply a V shaped equal bevel, I know that it was much used by swordsmiths in the early part of this century, though its main popularity was in the period known as shin-to, which is really coincident with the period from 1531 to 1865, almost a parallel of Tokugawa rule. I had better outline the specialist dating of the ages of swords, whilst it is still fresh in my mind, I will do so knowing that the ideals of study lie in persistence, ponder this well, as it is the power behind technique, but more of that later.

Kengyo

KIRI-ICHI-MONJI like the number one, which in Japanese is written as a horizontal dash, so too does this squared off tip. Many sword fans are of the opinion that a blade bearing such a tang tip has been shortened, it is also the prerogative of the Hosho line of the Yamato tradition, according to several sources.

Kiri-Ichi-Monji

A further source of intense debate are those of the filing of the tang to produce a particular shape and pattern indicative of that particular swordsmith and his tradition. Ninja would be aware of this form, it is suggested that messages were coded and filed into the tang of a sword, whereupon it would remain unnoticed, at the appropriate time it could be translated. I personally am sceptical of this practice, and have not seen any supporting evidence to further this theory. In any case the extremely old blades are devoid of any discernible file marks due to the extreme age, but also due to the fact that in former times a tang may have been shaped by shaving with a special tool known as a Sen.

Neither time nor space allows further in-depth discussion concerning file marks, save to say that the most ornate was known as Kesho-Yasuri and is literally the "full-dress" in terms of usng many conflicting directions of filing. It is very popular on swords manufactured in recent years. The hole that allowed the blade to be affixed to the tang is known as the mekugi ana. Several holes may occur upon a tang, this may be due to the sword being shortened at some time, or to the sword being mounted on different styles of what we call "koshirae", that is to say the complete style of mounting of handle and scabbard. Contrary to popular opinion a number of rivet holes (mekugi-ana) on a blade simply does not mean that a blade is of extreme age or quality.

Kesho-Yasuri

Now let me explain the periods we refer to in the study of swords. They are really quite simple:—

KOTO
SHINTO
SHIN-SHINTO
GENDAI-TO

Strictly speaking, there are many subtle variations of opinion as to what exactly constitutes the precise dating of the sword periods, depending upon who one's teacher was in the study of sword appraisal, or the opinion of one's master Tō-shō (swordsmith), but as a general course of study I would operate the give or take ten years either way dating system.

THE KOTO (Old Sword) period may be said to include the age of antiquities and the Dolmen burial mound swords of the second century B.C. right up to the mid to late 1500's. During this period, most of the major design and manufacturing details were evolved. I suppose that really we have been trying to get back to this purity. Swordsmiths as a race are notoriously bad keepers of records. Personal instructional manuals from this period are almost non-existent, due to the nature of the times, and the almost obsessive secrecy which a swordsmith worked under; many went to their graves, their secrets of forging dying with them, because a suitable successor did not appear.

THE SHIN-TO (New Sword) period lasted from the early 1600's to the second decade of the 1700's with the lack of any large scale battles for the Samurai to fight in, save the routine mopping up of some of the Tozama (outer lords — those who did not side with Tokugawa Iyeyasu at the Battle of Sekigahara — 1600 and the summer and winter Osaka campaigns of 1614-15, armed struggle on the grand scale had ended. Sadly, so too had the skill for producing practical swords. There are many records and manuals from this time, but they leave a sadness in the spirit. My thoughts go again to the work of Tō-Shō Kobayashi, who has definite opinions of this period, and the swords produced during it.

THE SHIN-SHINTO (recent sword) period, from about 1720 to 1865 an age of mass production of swords, factories grew up to service the Samurai, who had little to do but discuss old times. Also the rising merchant classes required pretty looking blades, in fancy mountings, with few exceptions a sorry time.

THE GENDAI-TO (Modern Sword) period from mid 1860's to the present day, is characterized with the tremendous upsurge in interest in the old ways.

It is indeed an exciting time, for I believe we are close to rediscovering many of the "lost" secrets of the Koto-period. What a mystery to forge the links in steel, with the masters long dead. In a strange way their spirits live on in the rediscovery of the subtle principles enshrined in the Japanese sword. How then does this apply to the Ninja you may ask, did not the Ninja have their own swords which were shorter and cruder than the swords that we see today. As I stated right at the beginning of this chapter, I cannot make any valid comment upon the modern expression of the Ninja, whether in film or theatrical production. The truth as always, is far far stranger. In my experience, as I have stated in my book upon shuriken-jutsu, all the major feudal ryu contained Ninja teachings within their curriculum. It is from this standpoint that all my observations are made. I am not exactly stating that I do not believe that these characters did not exist, for by the very nature of their practice, they should not leave behind any traces . . . . be that as it may. In the many documents of the martial ryu, all across Japan, quite definite techniques of silent kenjutsu are described. It is this that I shall describe to you, as much as I am able, without betraying that special confidence which has been placed upon me. Much of what I shall describe has not been collated together before, some may regard it as secret. But before the Deva Kings; I swear that in no way shall I prejudice the okuden teachings, which are not to be transmitted to a non-member of the ryu. By the name of he who has the power of the all seeing eye under heaven, by divine inspiration (TENSHIN SHODEN) I vow only to describe that which shall not cause the deities to fall into disrespect. It would not be honourable for me to imply otherwise, I trust that the details contained in this work shall be accepted as such by all manner of folks.

2. THE SPIRIT OF THE SWORD

To understand the spirit of silent kenjutsu, it is necessary to immerse yourself in the mechanics of the production of a true Japanese sword. The manufacture of true Japanese swords, whether it took place in the prestigious confines of a Daimyō feudal Lord's castle, or in a shrine to the War God Hachiman, or secretly by night in the dark forest away from the eyes of men; the principles of its manufacture were the same. Here I make the stringent distinction between a superb cutting weapon, and a badly formed piece of iron which has a slight shape similar to the true Japanese sword. If the blade is not forged with the spiritual cooperation of the swordsmith, then it is nothing, a piece of worthless rust. This perhaps needs a little explanation.

In the times that we are talking about, when the Samurai ruled the land, and anyone not Samurai was as nothing, the belief in what we call the "kami" was strong in all facets of daily life; later researchers have called this practice "animism". By it everything has a soul, whether it be living creature, or a leaf upon a tree. Thus there were auspicious days (kichinichi) upon which many endeavours were begun, and completed. There was a natural order, in the growth and decay of all things, this bound up with the imported idea of Karmha (destiny) made for a climate of thought and action that were to say the least intensely superstitious. There were many sayings which explained the principles in a swift clear manner, the Tosa warriors had a favourite, which I present here in possibly imperfect translation "A Man's fate is a Man's fate, and Life is but an Illusion". It is recorded in many variations all across Japan, but this is my favourite. Another which displays the same feeling is "Life and Death are but an Illusion, just Act".

Shinto deity shrine to Kami of Stone Nature.

Shinto purified paper strips

The concept of the total act was as important to a Samurai as the right he bore to wear the twin swords. They were constantly reminded to be strong to serve their Lord, and to endure hardship. There is a saying amongst the warriors of the Kanto "The body is like iron, the harder you beat it, the stronger it becomes". As much of the Ninja training was undertaken within the confines of the ryu, then the same emotions were expressed.

Let us understand the principles of making a true Japanese sword, this is of course a simplified discussion, due to limitations of space, for an in-depth study of the manufacture of true Japanese swords, I would draw your attention to a work which is currently in preparation, it is called "The Art of Iron Fire and Stone" by Yasuhiro Kobayashi, it is published by Dragon Books, and will be available where you obtained this book. I have read the rough draft, and I heartily recommend it. I believe it to be the first complete text in English concerning the production and display of a true Japanese sword from the refining of the irons and ores to the complexities of forging the ultra sharp blade. A sword is made to cut well, not to be a pretty item for tourists to gawp at, so we must redress the trend for flashily mounted swords, returning to the 'shibui' (refined elegance) of earlier times – this is most important.

I will now briefly discuss the process of making the true Japanese sword, regardless of Samurai, or Ninja, the underlying principle is the same. A day before the forging is to begin, the Tō-Shō (swordsmith) purifies himself in the age old misogi way, by water and by austerity.

Swordsmith's ritual purifaction

Under a waterfall

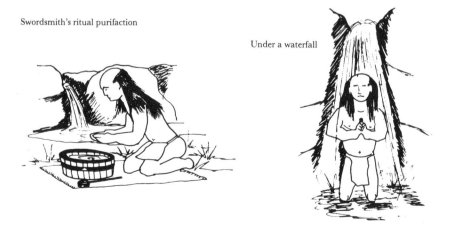

The Swordsmith dressed ready for the task

He has drawn away from the pleasures of the senses, even to the length of living in the smithy, he only eats a minimum of food essential to sustain life, and nothing that is of animal origin is eaten; usually plain boiled rice, or in lean times millet. The idea behind this is that the smith will not impart any of the "ki" of the dead animal into the sword. The smith then enters into a state of earthly grace, ideally it is the patron deity that will act through the smith's hands to create the blade. It is known that the swordsmith Sanjo Kokaji Munechika invoked the spirit of Inari Sama the fox spirit in the forging of the famous blade "Kogitsune-Maru" (Little Fox); according to tradition, the Fox Spirit appeared as a hammerman, in the guise of a young boy. It is said that Munechika refused the boy on the grounds that he was too small to lift the heavy long handled hammer, but the Fox Spirit in the form of the young boy lifted the hammer with ease. Whereupon Munechika knew that the 'kami' were present, and so went on to forge a sword of excellent quality.

Having purified both body, mind and spirit with this rigorous regime, the smith would wear the ceremonial hakama (split culotte) and kimono, usually in white; he would tie a lacquered hat on his head, which was the traditional badge of his craft and pause to pray before the deity seat (shrine) which every smithy contained. Thus armed and providing it was "kichi-nichi", lucky or auspicious day, he would blow air into the charcoal to bring up the heat to the precise colour. Traditionally the swordsmith does not use any aid in gauging the temperature, only allowing the colour of the charcoal to tell him

Deity Shrine

when the time is right . . . . this is one of the secrets that are being rediscovered by Tō-Shō Kobayashi.

Before picking up his tools the swordsmith would intone whatever incantation to his protecting deity was fit, then he would twist his hands into the 'ju-ji no in', and 'kanku-ji' finger symbols, cutting away the four poisons of doubt, greed, fear and lust. Now he would pick up his tools. If he was refining tamahagane, from fine dusty iron sand, he would spend much time in mixing his proportions correctly. (This is a major criticism of swords made after the Koto period, that too often "namban tetsu" or foreign iron was used resulting in a poor flawed blade.) Next, if he was forging a sword, he would order the junior assistant to prepare the charcoal (traditionally the charcoal came from a supplier, though certain smiths preferred to manufacture their own) for a katana blade it is usually about forty five sacks of charcoal. The assistant may start out the day in sparkling white ceremonial clothes, but by the end of the day he would be "kuro-oni" literally a little black devil (this refers to his charcoal covered face in the firelight of the

Mystic hands of swordmaking

Refining the iron sand

smithy). Whilst the junior assistant struggled with the heavy sacks of charcoal, breaking up the charcoal into regular sized pieces with a hammer, so that there would be no "hot" spots to mar the evenness of the blade; the more senior assistants would aide the Tō-Shō in his secret preparations. At the right moment, the swordsmith would introduce the iron into the fire, praying to the deity to guide his hand. The smith would draw the heated iron from the fire, placing it upon the square anvil, he begins with gentle strokes of his small hammer, to form the iron into a rough rectangle to this he adds by hammerwelding, a bar of rough iron. This now forms a paddle-shaped pan, which he can manoeuvre with ease; to this he adds more tamahagane of his own making, piling the paddle with it. This is then brought to the fire and

Folding the iron

"The Sahite" hammerman

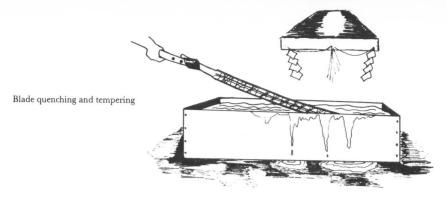

Blade quenching and tempering

gently heated up to the correct temperature, again by observing the colour of the steel and the fire. When the appointed time comes, he withdraws the glowing paddle, and beats it gently with his small hammer coaxing it into a rectangular block. (For precise details of this entire process, see Kobayashi-san's book.) The Sahite (senior assistant) raises his long handled hammer, and upon the command of his master, he begins to pound the iron block, varying the pace and the pressure on the unspoken command of the swordsmith. As you can imagine the apprenticeship for the senior hammerman is most thorough and exacting, there was a saying among the Yamato smiths, "a thousand men make a good hammerman". This means that only a rare sort of person is capable of seeing the course through to graduate as senior hammerman, and hopefully becomes a swordsmith in their own right. To paraphrase the English saying "Many are called, but few are chosen". Now assuming that we are referring to the so-called "kobuse" style of forging, whereby a soft iron core was wrapped around with a hard steel outer, at this point the swordsmith would take up

Tameshigiri and Suemonogiri

some soft grade iron and beat it into a shape roughly the same size as the paddle shape previously described, this would be set aside for a moment, whilst the first piece of iron was further worked. The popular name for this type of special work is "jumonji" simply that is a reference to the number ten (ju in Japanese), which looks like a cross, to make matters brief, this crossline is hammered into the piece of iron allowing it to be easily folded upon itself.

The two pieces of soft and hard iron are hammered together; this is difficult and much time and trouble is taken to ensure that no slag-ash is present in the metal. Similarly all air is excluded from the fold, otherwise the blade will "gas-blister" resulting in a weak blade. The resultant block is now hammered in a different way to elongate it into a rod, this is done several times to reduce the weight (see Tō-Shō Kobayashi's book for further information upon this subject).

By continuing the heating and hammering the classic shape of the Japanese sword is made. The curvature is worked upon, and the rough blade shape is now ready for scraping. The tool known as a 'sen' is used to make a scraped finish prior to filing. The filing, using coarse then semi coarse files, gives the final shape and a rough polish.

Now the art of the Tō-Shō (swordsmith) is really put to the test, he must temper the blade, to do this he mixes a special paste of iron sand, clay and charcoal (each smith would have his own "recipe") this would be coated all over the blade and allowed to dry a little. The next process was to scrape away certain parts of the clay, to allow the heat of the fire to get to different parts of the blade. The blade was then placed in the fire and heated again, at the right moment the whole blade was placed horizontally into a trough of warmed water, and thus the super hard edge of the Japanese sword was created. This edge is so sharp, so keen that it will easily cut through a steel helmet with little problem – in the skilled hands of a master swordsman of course. (For further discussion and illustration upon the arts of Tameshi-giri – cutting a fixed object and Iai Suemono-giri – cutting a bundle, please refer to my friend Mr Obata's book upon Toyama Ryu Batto-Jutsu, which is entitled 'Naked Blade' and published by Dragon Books.

Parts of the Japanese Sword
The Koshirae (sword style)

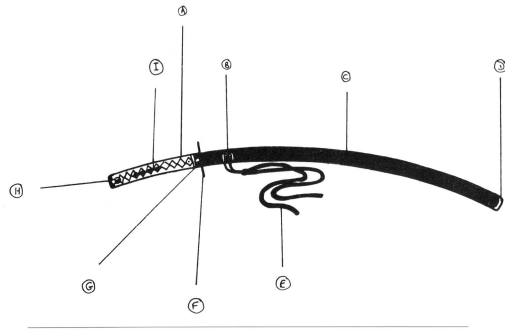

A	Tsuka	**D**	Kojiri	**G**	Fuchi-gane
B	Kurikata	**E**	Sageo	**H**	Kashira
C	Saya	**F**	Tsuba	**I**	Menuki

Parts of the Japanese Sword
Toshin – the blade

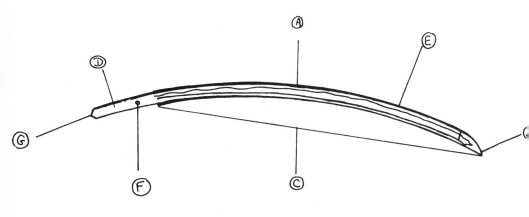

A	Ha	**D**	Nakago	**G**	Nakago-Jiri
B	Kissaki	**E**	Monouchi		
C	Nagasa	**F**	Mekugi-ana		

Partsof the Japanese Sword
Close up of blade

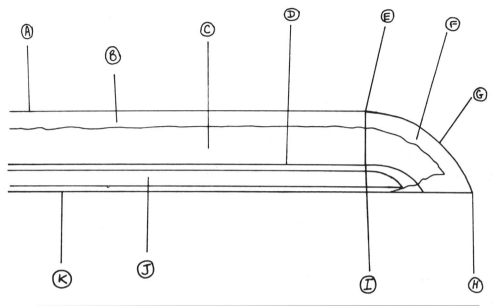

A	Ha	**E**	Yokote	**I**	Mitsukado
B	Hamon	**F**	Boshi	**J**	Hi
C	Ji	**G**	Fukura	**K**	Mune
D	Shinogi	**H**	Kissaki		

Parts of the Japanese Sword
Close up of the Tang

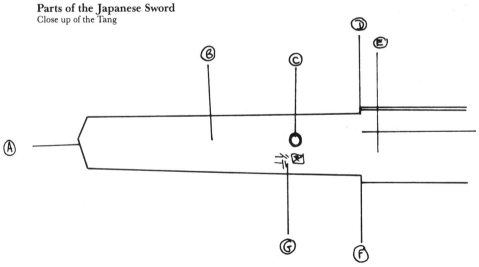

A	Nakago-jiri	**D**	Munamuchi	**G**	Mei
B	Nakago	**E**	Habaki moto		
C	Mekugi ana	**F**	Hamachi		

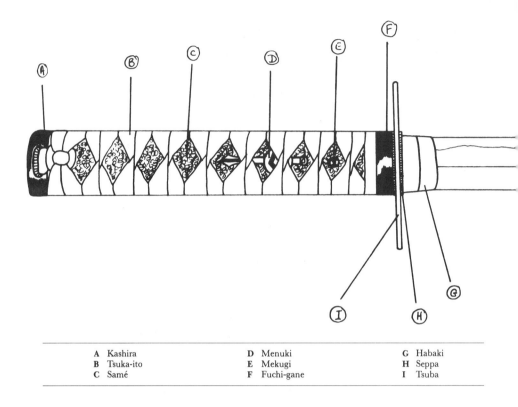

A Kashira	D Menuki	G Habaki
B Tsuka-ito	E Mekugi	H Seppa
C Samé	F Fuchi-gane	I Tsuba

The rough finished sword is known as "uchioroshi, in the past this was all that was necessary, for a battle sword, and I am of the opinion that this is as far as a Ninja blade would have gone, however with the lack of battlefield necessity, the look of the blade became more important than its cutting ability so the skills of the "togishi" (master polisher) came to be used. This was really the culmination of fine cosmetic work, but be careful not to judge a blade totally upon its outside appearance, the cosmetic skills of the togishi are many and great. It is often that a poor sword masquerades inside a fine exterior, the warriors of the Aizu-Han had a saying for this "see the fine fruit ripe and full, but inside the worm has eaten all the strength away". That is a little like life don't you think? Often the lofty idealists have no heart, and little spirit when put to the test.

Now it is necessary for you to know the parts of the Japanese sword, the following is a simplified list, which is suitable for basic study.

PARTS OF THE JAPANESE SWORD
(Japanese terms first, English second) – refer to illustration.

MI	The blade.
KISSAKI	Point of the blade.
YOKOTE	End of the Kissaki, extending to the Mitsukado.
SHINOGI	Ridgeline running both sides of the blade.
SHINOGI-JI	Area between the Shinogi and the Mune.
MUNE	Back of the blade.
HA	Tempered edge of the blade.
HAMON	Temper line.
HI	Groove running down blade.
HASAKI	Cutting edge.
HABAKI	Blade collar.
HABAKIMOTO	Area covered by the Habaki.
BOSHI	Outline of the Ha in the Kissaki.
JI	Area between the Ha and the Shinogi.
MUNAMACHI	Notch at the beginning of the tang.
NAKAGO	Tang.
NAKAGO-JIRI	Butt of the tang.
YASURI-ME	File marks on tang.
MITSUKADO	Meeting point of the Shinogi, Ko-shinogi and the Yokote.
KO-SHINOGI	Shinogi line in the kissaki.
FUKURA	Kissaki cutting edge.
JIGANE	Area between the Ha and the Shinogi.
MEKUGI-ANA	Peg hole in the Nakago.
MEKUGI	Bamboo peg which secures blade to handle.
KASHIRA	Butt-end of Tsuka.
TSUKA	Hilt.
FUCHI-GANE	Hilt collar.
TSUKA-ITO	Hilt wrapping.
TSUKA-MAKI	Classic "diamond shaped wrap".
KATATE-MAKI	"Battle" wrap.
SEPPA	Washers.
MENUKI	Hilt ornaments.
TSUBA	Guard.
SAME-MAKI	Ray-skin wrapping (Rhinobatus-Armatus).

SAYA	Scabbard.
TSUNAGI	Wooden blade.
SHIRA-SAYA	Resting scabbard.
KOJIRI	Butt-cap of Saya.
KOIGUCHI	Mouth of Saya (Carp's mouth).
KURIGATA	Cord knob (Half chestnut).
SORITSUNO	A scabbard clip.
KAESHITSUNO	A scabbard clip.
SAGEO	Sword cord.
NAGASA	Length from tip of Kissaki to Munamachi.
SORI	Curve.
MONOUCHI	Area of cutting (approximately seven inches from Kissaki).
SAKIHABA	Width of the blade at the Yokote.
MOTOHABA	Width of the blade at the Habakimoto.
FUMBARI	A blade that is wider at the Motohaba than the Sakihaba.
SUGUHA-HAMON	Straight temper line.
CHOJI-HAMON	Irregular temper line.
GUNOME-HAMON	Small pointed temper line.
SAMBONSUGI-HAMON	Triple point temper line.
YAKIBA	Tempered area.
NIE	Individual points of super hard steel.
NIOI	Misty line of super hard steel in Hamon.
KONIE	Small nie.
JI-NIE	Nie occurring in the Ji.
CHIKEI	Shiny lines in the Ji.
ASHI	"Legs" of super hard steel, projecting into the hamon at right angles.
YO	Detached leaf shapes of super hard steel.
SUNAGASHI	"Drifting sands" lines of Nie in the Ha.
KINSUJI	Shiny lines in the Ha.
INAZUMA	"Lightning" shaped lines in the Ha.
UTSURI	So-called "Bizen Double Yakiba" – a cloudy line bordering the Hamon.

So, now you have a veritable arsenal of terms, which I feel will help you greatly in your study of what shall, as you will see, become a study of great depth and importance; pause a while and ponder this. Remember one thing, there are those who will say that the Ninja did not use well forged blades, and they dismiss the subject, as though it did not exist. I offer the answer to this dismissal, is it possible that they do not know as much as they profess to know? . . . . It certainly is a theory which the thinking martial artist should research well, don't you think so?

It would be amiss of me not to conclude this chapter upon the Spirit of the Sword, without making a few points which may be of some help to the classical and modern exponents.

POINTS CONCERNING JAPANESE SWORD BLADES

First of all, it is absolutely useless to ask a sword collector for an opinion upon a sword blade, as he will necessarily be looking at it from the point of "Bijutsu" To-Ken, or as an art object. To use this criterion for choosing a blade for budo use, is about as dangerous as chambering a magnum load in a pistol that is not designed for it, the results are positively horrific to contemplate. (I wish to mention my old friend Mr. Kunishige, master of Ho-Jutsu (Musket arts) who suggested this comparison. In selecting a sword for serious budo use, and here I mean REAL budo use, it is necessary to have the advice of a high grade exponent in the arts to advise you. Above all do not try to use iai-to for real kenjutsu practice. The iai-to is the ultimate safe tool for the practice of IAI-DO, if you wish to progress further, then an alloy blade is not sufficient, nor for that matter is a type of sword which looks like a Japanese sword, but originates in Spain, it is a fine piece of workmanship to be sure, but for REAL practice it is not suited. I am not denigrating either the iai-to or the Spanish replica, they are both, in their way, fine items, but not suited to REAL practice. As a matter of course it is easy to purchase the former items. But a SHIN-KEN is a different matter, we are talking about a once in a lifetime expenditure, in excess of six hundred thousand Yen, or almost two thousand U.S. dollars at present exchange rates, so you see advice is most necessary.

For your information, what your advisor will be looking for is a very complex affair, but I will try to give you a slight insight into what he will be looking for.

First find a light source such as a pearl bulb.

Hold the blade at shoulder height, pointing tip towards the light.

Move your head, so that your eye is about two inches above the blade surface.

Look along it towards the light.

Move both your head and the blade to see the forging details.

If the angles are correct, then the blade will appear to be more or less evenly illuminated.

A long blade will have to be tipped down to reveal its entire light length.

No change must be seen in the surface.

The blade should be a pale glowing tone.

Tip the blade, and you will see a brilliant lit line running to the tip – this is the temper line, if you cannot see it then the blade is rubbish.

The shape of the line will depend upon the forging, and denote the school, this is where your advisor must use his judgement, some temper lines render a blade weak, so be careful.

Now you have found the temper line, you must be really careful, as I said before, the togishi (polisher) can work cosmetic wonders, you must watch out for this, it may not be done as a deliberate deceit, remember not every one who has owned a Japanese sword is interested in its correct usage. Some persons only want a pretty item, but often, as in life, that which seems finely dressed is really quite shallow, and falls apart when tested, I know that I have said this before, but it is so vital that you must make it a part of your heart, not only in this, but in all things. To make slight of this truly complex matter, I advise the following points to be taken into consideration:−

If in doubt . . . . . . Don't buy.
If the blade is dirty . . . . . . Don't clean, get advice.
If the blade is signed by a famous smith, forget it, you are concerned with the effectiveness, not the genealogy; also many blades are faked . . . . . . **Be careful!**

That really is all that is relevant in the scope of this book, we are really concerned with Ninja kenjutsu, if the reader wishes to proceed further, then I heartily recommend the two authors already mentioned in the text, Mr. Kobayashi and Mr. Obata, in their respective fields they are both most accomplished and will lead you on in a certain manner, if your desire is in that direction. Remember, "to ask is but a moment's shame, but to remain silent is a lifetime's shame".

Fuchi Kashira in
form of bats

Training is the preparation for practice, which is the forerunner of action. Action is the space between life and death . . . . Those of you who know my way of training will know that there is little to be gained by learning a mass of techniques too soon. It is my opinion based upon three decades of rigorous training, that that which is quickly achieved is quickly lost.

So let us proceed to construct the building blocks of what shall become a truly impressive skill, one that will outshine the ups and downs of everyday life. If you keep your heart resolute, then the problems which life sets upon you are but dust before the wind. Believe it, for it is true, I have proved this to be so, many many times . . . . Positive mind makes for positive action, this is a universal truth. If you truly believe that you will succeed, then what is there that can stop you? . . . . Believe it will be, truly; and it will be. Above all relax. Irrespective of whether you follow the classical, modern, or modern synthetic, this advice is relevant to you. I shall take for my example the type of training regimen that was fairly standard in the feudal ryu (school). Before a prospective student was accepted for entry into the deep mysteries that were the secret of the ryu. He would be subjected to a rigorous system of vetting, designed not only to find out if he was really suited to be a member of that ryu, but also, as was the nature of the times, his allegiance to the lord who was the patron of the ryu. In the case of the Ninja of the Kurama-Hachi-Ryu, much of the training of prospective students took place in the open air, in and around the densely wooded foothills of mount Kurama. It was reputed that great manhunts took place, in modern terms, much the same as the escape and evasion techniques taught to the modern Special Forces.

Prospective students would be told to travel north, for example, picking up certain items on their way. These things became progressively heavier, as the trek went on, and were of course designed to test the stamina and fighting spirit of a student. It was common for infringements of the beginners discipline to be punished by savage beatings, or being hung up by the wrists high up in the trees. Anyone who objected was obviously going to be a problem when in real combat a situation of life or death should occur.

It is a fact that huge pits filled with offal and other unpleasant substances were dug at regular points in the forest, the only way for a student to pass by a check area was to immerse himself in the filthy mire and virtually "swim" for it. This training, designed to desensitize a student, and strengthen his resolve is admirably demonstrated by the many cases of Ninja assassins hiding out in cesspits and other unpleasant areas. It is documented that several Samurai Lords were assassinated when attending to their personal hygiene, killed by Ninja hiding in the cesspit below the privvy. This of course is an extreme example of the lengths to which the true Ninja assassin would be prepared to go. For the relevance of this book however, I am not suggesting that anyone in this day and age should train themselves in this way, it is merely to illustrate that by correct grounding, the most noisesome of tasks can be endured and more to the point be successful. That is the important point. Now I suggest that before we discuss the actual practice of Kenjutsu, we begin, as they say, at the beginning.

This is now to introduce to you the position known as JIGOTAI.

Jigotai

Jigotai side view

31

To take up the posture of jigotai, first of all in the horizontal form, place your feet roughly one and one half shoulder widths apart, with the feet pointing outwards at forty five degrees, now as the old masters say, "Put power in your abdomen" and drop your weight downwards taking up the strain on the thighs. You should feel a pulling tension in the thigh muscle. Fans of karate-do are advised to study "Kiba-Dachi", or "Naihanchi-Dachi", there are some similarities, with the exception that the feet are not in the parallel plane. Now this horizontal jigotai is often called "ichimonji" jigotai, because of its similarity with the kanji (Chinese) character "Ichi" meaning number one.

It is said that a good posture creates a good character, so we must strive to perfect jigotai, remember as you make the posture, do not bend your back. Your head must be erect, and looking straight ahead. It may be of some assistance to you if you place your hands lightly in a cupping action on either side of your abdomen. Don't forget that traditionally this is the centre of your spiritual power, you must cultivate it at every opportunity otherwise that which is called Budo, is less than murder. Now begin by shaking off all doubts, this must be done in a serious manner. I advise that you practice this before going to your daily work. Arguments that there is no time in the modern world are nonsense, eighty years ago a student would walk ten miles to a dojo and ten miles from the dojo every day. That was normal. Have we become so weak? . . . . The answer lies with you does it not?

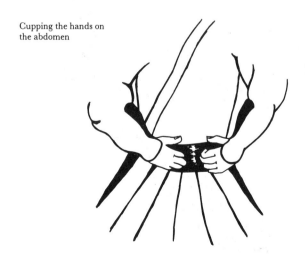

Cupping the hands on
the abdomen

This special jigotai method was once considered a secret training skill amongst the warrior monks atop Mount Hiei; there are those who say that it has a Chinese origin, and as such is bound up with the science of Chi-Kung. I am not so sure about this, but there are certainly ancient illustrations of monks performing similar postures to release, as they termed it "Iron Soul" – Tetsu-Shin. It is seen by many to be of misogi origin, which sets it amongst the practices of Shintoism. Whatever the case, I know that it is very powerful, if you persevere with it. It is said of jigotai, that as a foundation for the skill of kenjutsu it is without equal. For it is the object for the man to control the sword, and not the other way around. Research this point very thoroughly, it is of vital importance.

Warrior Monk

Warrior Monk with halberd

So, now on with the training:—

Assume ichimonji jigotai from the natural posture known universally as shizentai, as you do so emit a spirit meeting shout (kiai), this should be the sound of YAH! or TOH!, experiment to find which suits you best. Above all do not emit the shout from your chest or throat, try to use your abdominal wall muscles, to pull the diaphragm down. The resultant shout should resonate, making your stomach vibrate slightly, you may place your hands either side of your abdomen as stated previously. Now really feel this sound vibrate, if you cannot, then you must study harder, you are probably "chest breathing" as we say. This will cause a tightness in the chest, as the spirit cannot release itself fully. To counteract this, you must relax your shoulders and allow the stomach to swell out slightly. A word of advice to the body builders, a tight stomach saps strength and power, strong muscles are an armour to be sure, but constant tension constricts blood vessels causing poisons to accumulate. This is true no matter what form of healing you believe in, whether holistic or scientific. Now you have accustomed yourself to adopting ichimonji jigotai, whilst uttering kiai, you must school yourself to remain in the position of jigotai, even though you think your legs are on fire, and the muscles begin to shake, hold on, the rewards of such determination are marvellous, just be patient a little longer. Traditionally this was all a new student would learn for the first few months. Of course the fallout rate was extremely high due to the hardness of the method, but then, so it was supposed to be. Those who pass this stage are worthy of teaching, or so it was believed.

So now adopt ichimonji jigotai, emitting kiai, next thrust out both arms in front of you at shoulder height, now just wait, calmly breathing, that is all you must do. Just wait, soon you will tire of this and want to quit . . . . . . Don't, that is the mind trying to rule your spirit, be strong, hold on. Your arms will become like lead, but do not let them down, instead emit the kiai to strengthen your resolve. You must succeed, take each moment as it comes, don't wonder how long you have been stuck in this posture or you will give in, this is real battle, with an opponent superior to you . . . . . . your own mind. You must succeed! Of course at first your resolve will waver, and you will give in, but remember the old saying, "Today is the Victory over yesterday!" When you are thoughtless in this practice, and by that I mean that you can adopt the position and just stay there, you are then ready to progress to the next stage, this is accomplished as follows:—

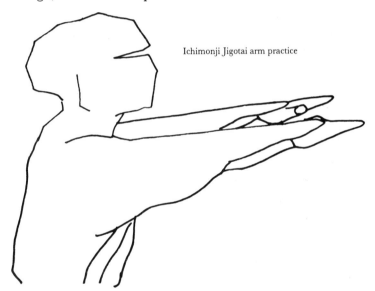

Ichimonji Jigotai arm practice

Assume ichimonji jigotai from shizentai, emitting the kiai and thrusting both arms out straight in front of you at shoulder height, now to the next stage and begin to clench your fingers into fists, you must clench very tightly, then release the grip spreading your fingers wide, wider still, then clench into fists. Repeat this again and again, you may shout to the timing of "Eh-Ho, Eh-Ho, Eh-Ho" and so on, just continue, with constant practice of this form you will come to be very aware of your lower abdomen, this is called "Tanden" or you may wish to refer to it as the "seat of power". The name does not matter, what is important, is that you are aware of it, the feeling is quite marvellous to experience, I urge you to persevere to experience it. But please remember, there is no "instant" Tanden awareness, such a concept is both sad and shallow, for it denies the great sacrifice that is necessary to enable a person to be truly, and strongly aware of this strength. This strength is the stuff of heroes, we have only to study the great Samurai and Ninja of the past, without exception they were devotees of the techniques of spiritual forging.

Ichimonji Jigotai finger clenching exercise

Having mastered the first form of ichimonji jigotai, you may study how to perform all the exercises in separate forms of jigotai, by moving forwards, backwards and sideways, you will see the sense in this later on, when you practice correct Kenjutsu.

So there is the practice known as "Happo-Jigotai, that is to say moving from Shizentai into Jigotai, whilst emitting kiai in eight directions. Before I detail Happo-Jigotai, let me explain the significance of the number eight. Eight was considered by the ancients to be myriad, that is expressive of universal law. The order of the universe idealised, becomes eight (in China the Ba-Gua and I-Jing -Pa Kua, and I-Ching respectively). All the ills of man were said to be influenced by the eight directions, and to placate them was a major part of early religion. This filtered into the Japanese Military as the science of Heigagku (from the Chinese geomancy known as Fong Sui), bearing this in mind, the Happo-Jigotai was believed to be a method of excorcising demons. Today we may use it to relieve stress that the modern society may place upon us.

HAPPO-JIGOTAI
Imagining oneself to be the centre of a compass (see diagram), with North (Hoku, Kita) in front of your face, as the ancients termed it.

Step obliquely north into migi (right) jigotai emitting kiai and bringing both hands sharply together in a smacking/clapping action. Retrieve back to shizentai.

Step back obliquely south (Nan, Minami) into hidari (left) jigotai, emitting kiai and slapping hands together as before. Retrieve to shizentai.

Step sideways west (Sei, Sai, Nishi) into ichimonji jigotai, emitting kiai and slapping hands together. Retrieve to shizentai.

Step sideways east (to, higashi) into ichimonji jigotai emitting kiai and slapping hands together. Retrieve into shizentai.

Step half-sideways into hidari (left) jigotai facing north west (Ken, Inui) emitting kiai and slapping hands together. Retrieve shizentai.

Step back half sideways into migi (right) jigotai facing south east (Son, Tatsumi) emitting kiai and slapping hands together. Retrieve into shizentai.

Step forwards (half) into migi (right) jigotai facing north east (Gon, Ushitora) emitting kiai and slapping hands together. Retrieve into shizentai.

Step back, half sideways into hidari (left) jigotai facing south west (Kon, Hitsujisaru) emitting kiai and slapping hands together. Retrieve into shizentai.

The cycle is complete, and as the ancients believed, all the minus

北
乾　艮
八卦
八荒
西　東
坤　巽
南

The directional principle of Happo Jigotai

The movements of Happo Jigotai

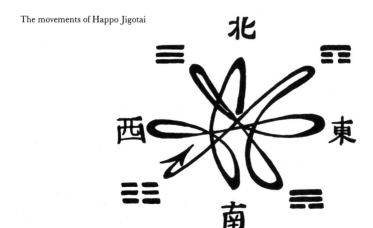

北
西　東
南

principles were eradicated. This is indeed a deep study, one that really warrants a complete volume to itself. For your reference the terminology referred to is also known as HAK-KE-Divinatory Trigram Method. This was once the special skill of the Shingon priests, though of latter times it has fallen into disrepute, beng treated as nothing more than a cheap amusement. Which is sad, as it's illustrious past was the underpin of the Empire.

Having strengthened the sinews through Jigotai methods, it is now important to practice seated meditation, this is the foundation of the HEI-HO (Secret Method). To master this is to become as the warriors of the Gempei Wars "Soul of the Mountain, Body like the freeflowing stream", that is to say strong of spirit and flexible of body and mind.

Traditionally the seated posture was Iai-Hiza, that is to say seated with one knee raised, I recommend this for both physical and mental stability, above all else, keep the top half of your body upright, as though there were a rod passing from heaven through to earth. Do not favour one side or the other. Clasp the hands together, intertwining the fingers and allow the middle fingers to point outwards at an angle of forty five degrees, the tips of the fingers must lightly touch. Place strength in the area of the tanden and close the breathing solidly as the old meditation masters were fond of saying. You must breathe in and out slowly and firmly, there are several methods which will be of use to you, it is up to you to chose the precise method that is suitable. If you study a method already, please ask the advice of your senior, as I do not wish to cause any dissention amongst fellow martial artists.

METHOD ONE I refer the following practice as being of the highest order. It stems from the Soto-Zen school of introspective mysticism. Seated in Iai-Hiza, with the "gaze of far distant mountains" (Enzan no Metsuke) begin to calm your spirit.

Breathing from the abdomen begin to intone the following, which is known as the heart sutra-Maka Hanya Hara Mitta Shingyo. I have split it up into the various syllables to aid easy chanting of its powerful form. As it really is a method for improving coordination of breathing,

I will not labour you with the deep significance, that truly would take several volumes to explain, but for your information, I will include a translation which may be of some interest to you.

Now, before we start, remember that as you say each syllable, it must be completed with even breath.

MA KA HAN NYA HA RA MITTA SHIN GYO.
Kan Ji Zai Bo Satsu Gyo Jin Nya Ha Ra Mi
Ta Ji Sho Ken Go On Kai Ku Do Issai Ku Yaku
Sha Ri Shi Fu I Ku Ku Fu I Shiki Shiki Soku
Ze Ku Ku Soku Ze Shiki Ju So Gyo Shiki Yaku Bu
Nyo Ze Sha Ri Shi Ze Sho Ho Ku So Fu Sho Fu
Metsu Fu Ku Fu Jo Fu Zo Fu Gen Ze Ko Ku Chu
Mu Shiki Mu Ju So Gyo Shiki Mu Gen Ni Bi
Zesshin Ni Mu Shiki Sho Ko Mi Soku Ho Mu Gen
Kai Nai Shi Mu I Shiki Kai Mu Mu Myo Yaku Mu
Mu Myo Jin Nai Shi Mu Ro

Shi Yaku Mu Ro Shi Jin Mu Ku Shu Metsu Do
Mu Chi Yaku Mu Toku I Mu Sho Toku Ko Bo
Dai Satta E Han Nya Ha Ra Mi Ta Ko Shin Mu
Ke Ge Mu Ke Ge Ko Mu U Fu On Ri Issai
Ten Do Mu So Ku Gyo Ne Han San Ze Sho Butsu
E Han Nya Ha Ra Mi Ta Ko Toku A Noku Ta Ra
San Myaku San Bo Dai Ko Chi Han Nya Ha Ra Mi
Ta Ze Dai Jin Shu Ze Dai Myo Shu Ze Mu Jo Shu
Ze Mu To Do Shu No Jo Issai Ku Shin Jitsu Fu
Ko Ko Setsu Han Nya Ha Ra Mi Ta Shu Soku
Setsu Shu Watsu.

GYA TE GYA TE HA RA GYA TEI
HARA SO GYA TE BO JI SO WA KA
HAN NYA SHIN GYO.

Iai-Hiza front and side views

THE HEART SUTRA

Now when the Bodhisattva Kannon was practicing the profound Hara Mitta Shingyo he saw all before him to be emptiness, and so passed beyond suffering.

Oh, my disciple, form is not different from emptiness, emptiness is not differrent from form; form is emptiness and emptiness is form; and so also is sensation, thinking, impulse and consciousness. All these things have the character of emptiness, neither born nor dying, neither defiled nor pure, neither increased nor lessened.

So in emptiness there is neither form nor sensation, thinking, impulse nor concentration; no eye, ear, nose, tongue, body nor mind; no form, sound, smell, taste, touch nor object of mind; no element of eye, nor any other of the other elements, including that of mind consciousness, no ignorance and no extinction of ignorance, nor any of the rest, including age and death and extinction of age and death; no suffering, no origination, no stopping, no path; no wisdom and no attainment.

Close up of hand position

The Bodhisatva, since he is not gaining anything, by the Hara Mitta Shingyo has his heart free from the net of hindrances, and with no hindrances in the heart there is no fear. Far from all perverted dream thoughts, he has reached ultimate Nirvana. By the Hara Mitta Shingyo all the Buddhas of the three worlds have the utmost, right and perfect enlightenment. Know then that the Hara Mitta Shingyo is the great spiritual Mantra, the great radiant mantra, the supreme mantra, the peerless mantra, which removes all suffering, the true, the unfailing. The mantra of the Hara Mitta Shingyo is taught thus:

Gone, Gone, Gone beyond, altogether beyond,
Awakening, Fulfilled!

I think you will agree that this is indeed a profound statement for a true martial artist to ascribe too, whether he be classical, modern or even modern synthetic, so the wisdom placed down almost fourteen hundred years ago comes down the ages.

To echo Prince Arima's words in the Manyoshu.

Iwashiro no	*On the beach of Iwashiro,*
Hamamatsu ga e wo	*I pull and knot together*
Hikimusubi	*The branches of the pine.*
Masakiku araba	*If my fate turns out well,*
Mata kaerimimu	*I shall return to see them again.*

Of course I realise that this method may be a little too severe for the beginner, so I offer the following simplified method:

Assume Iai-Hiza, lock the hands together as described.
Breathe in slowly for a count of ten, pause for a count of five, then breathe out for a count of ten pause then repeat the cycle.

Ten minutes, then twenty and so on everyday will bring amazing results. This is the truth of training, "One drop of water starts an ocean. One grain of sand begets a mountain".

4. SILENT KENJUTSU

Now before I explain precisely what the Ninja Sword Art of Silent Kenjutsu is, I propose to tell you exactly what it is not. First of all, at its heart it is not a means of self perfection, (a Do way) this it certainly is not. It is certainly not a means of entertainment, regardless of how members of the acting profession have portrayed it through the years.

It has no sporting outlet.
It is not a means of improving social classes.
If then it is not all of these things, what is it?

The answer is simple. It is the art of cutting down an adversary — instantly. Now usually the precise distinction is made, for sporting or for political reasons of the separateness of Kendo to Iai-do; or of the differences between Iai-Do and Iai-Jutsu. Batto-Jutsu to Kembu etc. etc.

Now in my interpretation of things, the many and varied forms of sword play which the feudal Ninja would know, depended directly upon his Clan allegiances and/or his membership of a particular martial ryu. Thus for example a Kenshi (Master) of the Kurama Hachi-Ryu would respond to a given situation in a totally different form to say, one who had trained in Muso Jikiden Eishin Ryu, but then that was the reason for the differences in the ryu. It has been accurately documented that at one time there were well over five thousand separate ryu, a high percentage of which contained within their curriculum the techniques that we have come to refer to as Ninjutsu. We must, for the sake of classical purity make the distinct separation of battlefield techniques, which involved a considerable social form. For example prior to a fight between Samurai at the Battle of Kyoto which took place on the night of the twenty ninth of July 1156, the incident is described by the Hogen Monogatari thus:

The warrior Tametomo is challenged by two opposing Samurai,

> *"We are Oba Kageyoshi and Saburo Kagechika, honourable descendants of the great Kamakura Gongoro Kagemasa, who, when he attained the age of sixteen years in the three years war of Hachiman Taro (Minamoto Yoshiie) at the attack made upon the Castle of the Kanazawa in Dewa Province went out before all others, at the head of the battle line and was hit in the eye by an arrow . . . . The arrow tore out his left eye and left it hanging upon the side plate of his helmet, but so brave was he that he sent an arrow in reply and killed his enemy. We, his descendants seek redress and challenge you".*

This is one of the shorter preambles to Samurai fighting upon the battlefield. The reason for this is plain, the Samurai did not wish to fight with a social inferior, and at the same time did not wish to fight with a superior, thus the battlefield was an ordered affair. Now that was

Battlefield formalities

Gekokujo

fine until the Ashigaru spoiled it all with the terrible Gekokujo which meant that they would attack anything, often on their own side, it was labelled as the "low oppress the high" by many writers of the period.

Now then, what was the ideal of Ninja Kenjutsu? . . . . Simply – drawsword, strike to kill, get away, – simple as that. Often this was brought about in a crowded area, so that no one knew what had happened until it was too late, the target had been killed and the Ninja was safe. Or at night on a battlement, a Lord gazes up at the night sky, before he has registered the sound, a sword has drawn and cut his head off, and the attacker is making good the escape before the Lord's lifeless body hits the ground.

Strictly speaking, I suppose it would be more correct from one standpoint to call the action Iai-Nuki, or simultaneous strike, but that is to minimise the complexity of the practical side of the form.

Usually the target was unaware of the impending attack, in true pre-emptive strike style a target would be locked into and the deed effected so quickly that it has been named by one more poetic writer as "The whisper of the dragonfly", though why this simile has been drawn eludes me. Despite this it is referred to as such in several Emaki of the Old Ryu. So I will bow to their superior knowledge. If a future researcher has the answer to this I would be most grateful to know his opinion.

Now when battle was joined and a fight was unavoidable the skills of true Ninja Kenjutsu came to the fore. For every situation, a special skill had been worked out, this was common to all the ryu. Thus the sum total of many generations was crystallised into the supremely

Ninja uses silent Kenjutsu

effective fighting form. One thing that the Ninja form of Kenjutsu had which differed greatly from the Samurai form, was that the Ninja could easily run away when an opportunity arose. A Samurai, because it would mean loss of face could not and so would die where he stood. For the Ninja however, there was no such distinction, for even if he was a Samurai retainer in his normal life, once engaged on a mission all his past life was forgotten and he reacted as was expected of "Hinin" – literally "Non Human", which in the case of the full time "Career Ninja" is the strata of feudal society from which the Ninja came.

To understand fully the complexities of Iai-nuki – the simultaneous strike, we must understand the mechanics of the ryu that evolved the Sword drawing form. According to tradition the Ninja forerunners – the Tengu (Winged demons) were the first to codify the arts of the Sword. There is the well known almost certainly apocryphal story, concerning the Tengu teaching the famous Hero "Yoshitsune" how to "drink hot water" as their skill was referred to. It is said that Yoshitsune went on to be the greatest hero in Japan, along with his friend the man mountain Benkei, and they had many adventures.

Remember that a silent blade along the line of an artery allows a quick kill and an even quicker escape.

Yoshitsune

There are four elements that must be researched deeply into, they are in simple terms, the elements of IAI.

The four basic principles

> NUKI-UCHI *Draw and strike*
> KIRIOROSHI *To strike down an opponent*
> CHIBURI *To cleanse a Blade*
> NŌTŌ *To return a sword to its scabbard*

The essence of true practice, as the ancient Ninja warriors said, was that of warugashiko, or cunning.

EXPLANATION OF WARUGASHIKO

To cut a man down cleanly, is a skill of great accomplishment. This must be done with an honest heart, free of selfish desire, but in this way, we must also exhibit warugashiko. This cunning is not to be confused with the desire of selfish men, that cunning is resultant in the destruction of the true heart.

As an example of this, I cite the case of a retainer of the Kato, Lords of the Mizoguchi Clan from Omi province in the north west of the Iga region. Gompachi was a thirteenth class Samurai, more at home with his books than the Sword. One day Gompachi was returning to the records house, when his way was blocked by a young Ronin (masterless samurai). The warrior was unkempt in his appearance, and clearly looking for trouble. With his way barred, Gompachi could not turn back, and against such an obvious rough, he could not go on.

The rough warrior drew his sword and brandished it, in fast movements, inviting Gompachi to a duel. The result was obvious, Gompachi would die.

Here then, Gompachi exhibited warugashiko, he said to the rough, that he saw that he was against a master warrior, and that he was as good as dead, so he would like to give the warrior his sword to keep, before he was cut down. The rough warrior was flattered and sheathed his sword, ready to take Gompachi's sword, whereupon Gompachi drew his sword nuki-uchi style and cut the rough's head cleanly off. From that day onwards, gentle Gompachi was known as "Gompachi-Hakujin" (Gompachi the drawn sword). I think his story explains what warugashiko is about.

Let us now understand in depth all the elements of true swordsmanship.

NUKI-UCHI must be practiced very slowly, there must be no sound as the blade leaves the scabbard. Look at the koi-guchi of your scabbard (mouth of the scabbard), if it is cut about, then you are not drawing cleanly or smoothly. That is why it is best to practice in a quiet place, where you can hear even the slightest rasping sound. It is important to make silence, that means that all the parts of the cutting edge of the sword as it exits the scabbard are away from the scabbard. This is most important, a carelessly drawn blade is capable of cutting through the scabbard entirely, inflicting a crippling wound to the hand. True Nuki-Uchi is a simultaneous strike from a sheathed position; to be effective, it must be silent . . . . remember that.

So too, the rest of the techniques of the sword drawing and fighting method; must be silent.

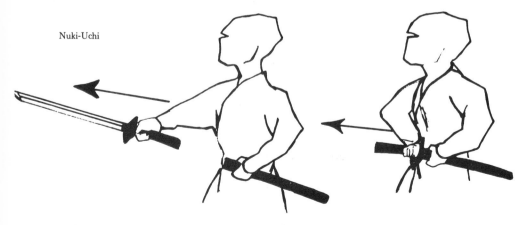

Nuki-Uchi

KIRIOROSHI is difficult to perform silently, but this must be the case, otherwise the enemy will expect an attack and counter it. It is the slow blade that cuts cleanly, do not confuse this with the fast blade of Iai-Do and Jutsu. It is important to make slight action effective, it is considered a great skill to be able to cut through many straw bundles (see Mr Obata's book). This is true to be sure. It was also considered a great skill to be able to dispatch an enemy using only two inches of the Mono-Uchi (cutting edge), rather than using eight inches or more.

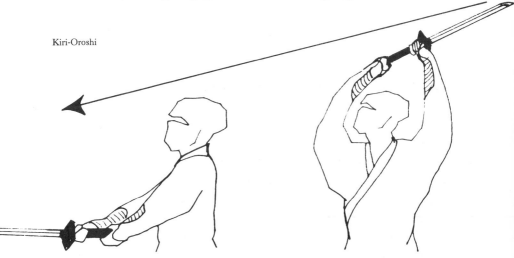

Kiri-Oroshi

CHIBURI (blood shake) or **CHI-NUGUI** (blood wipe) is performed in an unreal method. No warrior is going to place a soiled blade in his scabbard merely after shaking it in the air (of course this discounts the technique of simultaneous draw, cut, sheathe mentioned elsewhere). It is important to thoroughly cleanse all edges of all waste matter.

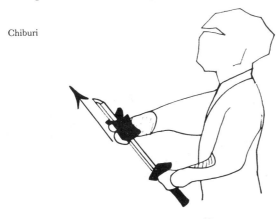

Chiburi

NŌTŌ is the action of returning the sword to its scabbard. It is performed silently, do not mimic actors in the motion pictures, they are not true swordsmen in the classical sense, and their example is only for the purposes of entertainment. At the height of greatest skill; it is desirable to replace the sword with the same speed that it exited, but this is very much a matter of experience, be warned against too swift a progress, it is possible to severely injure oneself by carelessly returning the sword to its scabbard. Remember above all else, that the height of martial skill in the classical sense is true silence. Silent Kenjutsu is but one expression for an attitude of mind, spirit and body, I urge you to experiment to reveal its truth to you, for nothing is achieved by laziness, or despondency.

Have courage, endure the hardship and arrive at true "Silent Kenjutsu".

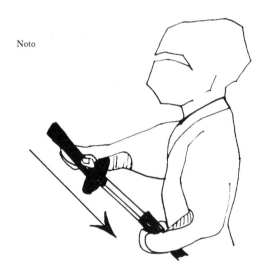

Noto

5. ANATOMY OF CUTTING

The ultimate test is in the execution of the technique, not against air, or straw bundles, or bamboo; but against a living target. That is why, to repeat myself, Ninja Kenjutsu had no sporting outlet, and was not concerned with spiritual development other than becoming an effective weapon. This is of course from the classical feudal standpoint, and no aspersions are cast against any person or organisation, whether past present or future and their interpretation of what constitutes "Ninjutsu".

To the feudal Ninja the paramount skill to learn was anatomy, this was often accomplished incognito as an inquisitor at one of the execution grounds, which were a vital part of any castle town, more as a deterrent to insurrection than actual punishment. To the feudal Japanese mind, only a guilty person would be apprehended by the forces of correction. Thus it was a simple manner to mete out the appropriate sentence . . . . . Death. In the early days, this could be by crucifixion, beheading, spearing, burning, boiling, slow strangulation, poisoning, disembowelment, drowning, suffocation, skinning alive, and many other well documented forms, including being buried alive up to the neck and inviting passers by to take kicks at the head. This terrible end is documented to have befallen Ishida Mitsunari, once proud Lord of Osaka Castle and influential member of the coun-

Execution ground

cil of Regents, which governed the land prior to 1600. After a lifetime of unspeakable violence, this, some may say, appropriate end, came as a result of losing to General Tokugawa Iyeyasu.

For the apprentice Ninja, there was no stigma or shame attached to the skills of the executioner/inquisitor, indeed there was a pride in a job well done. As a point of information, during the bloody Shimbara revolt of 1638, the feudal lord (Daimyo) Matsukura Shigeharu had a particularly gruesome way of despatching his peasant enemies, who after all were only Christians. The method which his executioners used, was to tie the unfortunate person with hemp bindings, and then tie onto them a straw rain cloak, which was soaked in fuel oil. The straw was set alight and the burning bundles allowed to run around, until death overtook them, much to the amusement, so it is documented of the Daimyo Matsukura. It is rumoured that the Mito Ninja had connections with this vile ruler. It has been suggested, but as yet not been proven conclusively, that the Mito Ninja used the execution ground at Shimbara for training in the late 1585-6 winter assault.

So much for the background of the times, suffice it to say that it was not a time to be born without the natural will to survive, truly the

length of a man's life was as long as his sword arm.

Which brings me to the subject of sword testing, usually when a sword was made, it was required that the sword be tested by a professional sword tester. Such tests took place again in the execution grounds of the great castle towns. Indeed the Yamada family refined the testing of swords and spears to something resembling a fine art. They left their discoveries in a fifteen part scroll, which became the standard reference work for a person wishing to know how to strike with a sword. It was this intense study of Ha-Suji, the precise blade attack angle that singled out the Yamada for particular notoriety. It is well documented that young Samurai would travel incognito to learn the secrets of the Yamada. One such student upon asking how to cut was told to build a mound of wet sand approximately his waist height and to practice cutting, full force in excess of three thousand cuts before dawn and a thousand after dusk, the main part of the day being taken up with his duties as "Honourable corpse setter". Many young Samurai were recruited, in secret of course, as the skill of the sword tester marked him out as "Eta" in the social order (similar in many respects to "Hinin").

This state of affairs is well documented, indeed the photographer Felix Beato, who was one of the first Westerners to enter Japan with a camera, photographed the "Honourable head-taker" of Edo (present day Tokyo) in his execution yard, this date, sometime around 1865-66 according to the Beato Estate also notes that the executioner's pay was 5 to 7 Ichibu per head, and it was a conservative estimate to say he would take at least 350 heads in one year.

The major rivals to the Yamada Family, were the Nakagawa, the headmaster of which, one Sahioda Shigeuki, dearly wanted to take the title of executioner under the patronage of the Tokugawa family. He was almost manic in his attempts to outshine the Yamada in his skill in Tameshigiri, even to the extent of writing a rival training manual, which went into the preciseness of the executioners' mental state, almost trying to elevate it to the status of an art form; however his social class was against him, and he always remained the second placer to the Yamada.

It is interesting to note that of the workers who were regulars at the various execution grounds, there would be regular unexplained absences, it has been suggested that this was due to their services being required, shall we say as "sub-contractors" to a feudal Lord who required that special service that the professional executioner could provide.

Whilst it may be a fact that is not generally favoured, it must be said, that by the time of the Mid-Tokugawa period, the average Samurai did not know how to use a sword at all, indeed it was in the best interest of the Bakufu (Tokugawa government) to ensure that the vast array of Samurai were not "battle ready". This was simple logic, which would preserve peace. So, if a Lord wished to remove a rival, he had the choice of Ninja, which at this time would have been difficult as most of the Ninja had been drawn into the service of the Tokugawa Metsuke (all seeing eyes).spy network; or else would be untrustworthy, or the alternative of hiring an execution ground worker. But this was a vicious circle, for the worker may have been a Ninja "sleeper", quietly biding his time and improving his skill. It was very much a case of trial and error.

The honourable corpse-setter

Beato and the head-taker

Yamada Asaemon

Dodan-Nuki

Ninja climbing wall

The third major school which drew aspiring "cutters down" was that of the Chokushi. The Chokushi school was founded by the illustrious Moriyama Shosho Minamoto no Yorisada, who was the direct pupil of Nezu Saburobei no Jo Mitsumasa; Moriyama also left his skills to posterity in the form of a diary of working notes, which he named "Chokushi ryu Tameshi mono no Maki"

It may sound barbaric in these present "enlightened" times, but in the act of cutting down, great importance was paid to the way that the various tissues and fats adhered to the blade, and what tone the sword blade was discoloured by the blood (thus making an absolute nonsense of the practice known as "Chiburi" or "Chi-Nugui", which is the practice in Iai-Do of returning the blade to the sheath-ready position of nōtō by mimicking the removal of blood by a slight shake or wipe). It is reported that in the days of Yoshimune 1717-1745, the Shogun demanded that any of his blades that had been submitted to the cutting test, be brought to him immediately without being cleaned, that he might observe the discolouration and possible weakness in the blade that would be masked by the cleaning and light cosmetic polish, normally done before showing a blade to its owner. Apparently as exalted a person as Shogun Yoshimune was admonished by one of his advisors, who's stomach was disturbed by the blood-stained Sword. With all the resolve of his proud forebear Tokugawa Iyeyasu, Yoshimune looked sternly at the equerry and said "In the science of Budo, there is nothing tarnished or filthy; tense your stomach and be a man". It is not documented what became of the equerry, but it was a severe admonition by the standards of the Shogun's court. Men had been known to commit ritual suicide (Seppuku) for far less than this.

There were precise rulings laid down by the Tokugawa Shoguns, concerning the type of persons who were liable to be cut down in the execution grounds, and later used for sword testing. As a general rule, any person who was "shorn of hair" (head shaved) was exempt, this included Samurai, Doctors, holy men of either the Shinto or Buddhist Religions, and strangely any person tattooed with a religious subject such as guardian deities or a Bonji, which to answer the puzzle, are the chapter headings used in The 'Ninja Star – Art of Shurikenjutsu'. Basically bonji were of Sanskritic or Bali origin, and are very old, originating in India with Bodhidarma (Daruma), in Japan they are bound up with Shingon Mikkyo, and with the old earth mother fertility rites. Their power is dismissed today as being "just a load of hocus-pocus" but I will reserve judgement, as their effectiveness in the country villages against the madness known as "fox-possession", is almost ninety five percent effective. To return to the job in hand, persons who had skin cancers (carcinoma) were also not allowed to be used in testing of blades.

Now assuming the aspiring Ninja "cutter-down" had learned his lessons well at the execution ground, he was passed up in grade to a level of immediate field operative, as they say in modern business, that is to say he, or she, for the Kunoichi (female ninja) could observe at a distance, though not actually take part in the execution ground work, as it was done wearing only fundoshi loincloths, because of the blood; would be proficient to take out on an assassination mission of a civilian.

Ritual Seppuku

Inspecting the blade

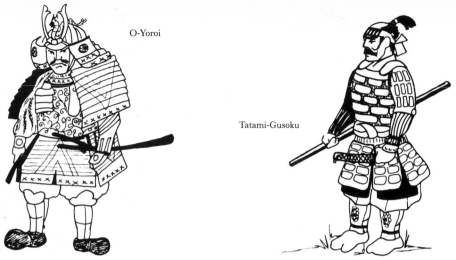

O-Yoroi

Tatami-Gusoku

If as occurred on countless occasions in the time of the warring states – pre 1600, it was necessary to kill a Samurai who was dressed in full armour, then a drawn out skirmish between Ninja and Samurai, would probably end in the Ninja death, due to the fact that at the time of the warring states, Samurai skill in use of the practical sword was at a height that has never been surpassed. So in true Ninja fashion, it was necessary to use guile, or at least mob the Samurai in the style of geko-kujo (low oppressing the high). Oh, and may I say something about Ninja on the battlefield, they did not wear the black cover-all, which is often depicted on T.V. The reality is that they would wear armour of the same clan as the person they were to assassinate. Which returns me to the second method whereby a Ninja could fight against a Samurai in broad daylight, that was to become a pupil of a maker of Katchu-armour. The idea being that to exploit the anatomical knowledge learned at the execution ground, was useless, if the area attacked was heavily armed; which by the way is the purists' criticism against modern Kendo practice; that it teaches attacks to an area that is already heavily defended by armour.

So the aspiring "cutter-down" would work for a master armourer, possibly even the elevated Myochin family, who it is recorded, had over one hundred and fifty one pupils, who in turn founded families of armour makers, the surmise that there were not just a few "sleepers" among that tremendous amount of skill, is to say the least-likely. With the knowledge of the weak points of all the major styles of armour from the folding Tatami Gusoku, to the Musket proof Yukinoshita-Do, and the archaic O-Yoroi battle armours of a previous age, the Ninja could justifiably refer to himself as "cutter-down".

Yukinoshita-Do

Battlefield Ninja

To kill with a sword, with one cut is for most men, even high grade Budo-ka difficult, if not impossible. To hack around and create much blood and distress to both parties is easy . . . . any fool can do it. But to kill, with the sword, single handed or double handed, silently and quickly is what I mean by Silent Kenjutsu . . . . I urge you to research this point in depth. Before I catalogue, what is in reality the way to kill with the sword, I must stress upon all readers, whatever their persuasion may be, that these are antique techniques, we have no need for them as we enter the twenty first century, but they are important, as they have allowed us to progress this far. As a matter of sociological study, they are just as important, in their own way as the paintings of Sesshu or the magnificent shrines of Ise and Izumo, for without them, history as we know it would have been a vastly different affair.

For those of you who are intrigued by the arts of true swordsmanship, I have some advice. In Japan at this moment, it is felt that there is a lack of competent instructors of true swordmanship. Modern tameshigiri is a fine and skilful art, but if the method of instruction is erroneous, then modern tameshigiri can give a brutal impression upon an onlooker. This situation has been helped by the inaugeration of the All Japan Batto-Do Federation, which sets a standard, nationwide, whereby students no matter what their school may progress in a safe and sure manner, polishing their art into a wondrous thing to behold. This is true modern tameshigiri, I urge you to study this deeply. For your information the modern tameshigiri is performed with correct etiquette upon bamboo or straw targets, and is an endeavour of spiritual improvement.

For those of you outside Japan, I heartily recommend my friend Mr Obata. He is an accomplished teacher in the true Tameshigiri method, and is very caring and careful for foreign students.

So, let us return to a situation, possibly three hundred years ago, now it is obvious to anyone with an ounce of intelligence, that to go up against a trained fighting machine, which is what the feudal Samurai was, and fight against him, trading blow for blow, was to invite entry to heaven's gate. For an armoured man, the attack areas were:—

Against O-Yoroi; *(Great Armour) of the Fourteenth year of the Eleventh Century, prior to the era of Tenki*

1 Under the Sendan No Ita and up into the central chest cavity.

2 Through the gap of the Makko no Hazure and the Fukiga-yeshi into the temple.

3 Between the Sode and the Kyubi no Ita into the armpit, and heart.

4 Through the Yurugi-Ito from the front to the intestinal area.

5 Through the Yurugi-Ito from the rear to the spinal column (between the Koshi no O).

Please refer to Armour illustration No. One.

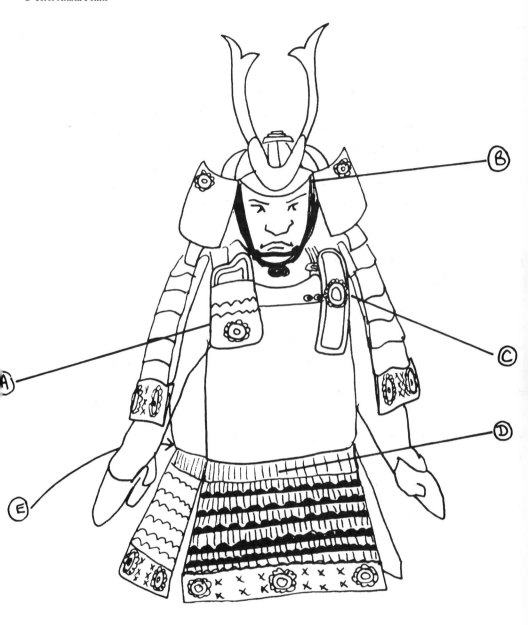

A	Sendan No Ita	**D**	Yurugi-ito
B	Gap between Mako No hazure & Fuki Gayeshi	**E**	Rear Yurugi-ito between Koshi No O
C	Between sode & Kyubi No Ita		

Against Tosei Gusoku *of the mid Keicho period (late 16th century)*

1 Above the Abiki no O and below the Kohire to the front of the armpit.

2 Through the Hikiawase to the lungs. Or armpit.

3 Between the Gesan or Kusazuri and up at the front to the intestines.

4 Between the Gesan or Kusazuri and up at the back to the spinal column or the kidneys.

5 Just above the Waki-Ita into the armpit.

Please refer to armour illustration No. Two.

So you see from a gap of some six hundred years in the development of Japanese armour, to the skilful Ninja, the same mistakes of design were made. I tentatively ask, were these mistakes deliberate? . . . . Think about it. Now to my mind there were only a few attack paths for the Ninja.
They were quite simply:—

> Innerside of arm
> Armpit
> Wrist-pulse side
> Lower intestine
> Spinal column
> Groin
> Inner side of upper thigh
> Back of knee

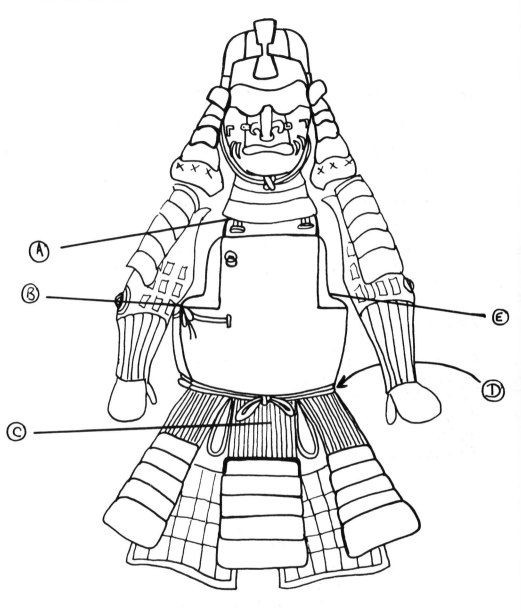

A	Above Abiki No O & below Kohire	**C**	Between Kusazuri (Gesan)
B	Through Hiki Awase	**D**	Between rear Kusazuri
		E	Above the Waki-Ita

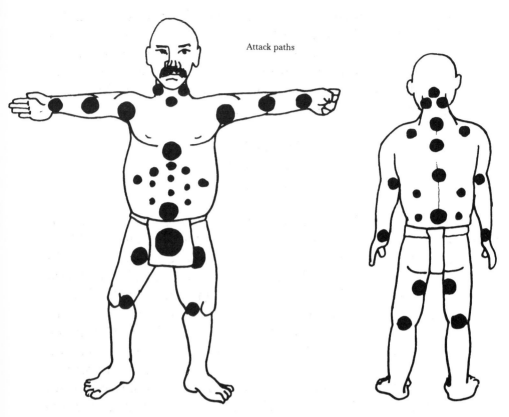

Attack paths

Any or all of these areas were relatively easy to attack, particularly for a person with advance knowledge of the construction of Japanese Armour. They all correspond with a major grouping of veins, arteries, or nerves, and as such were known to be consistently effective, as either killing, or disabling cuts.

For the Ninja operating against a person not wearing armour, all the previous areas, plus several others were attackable; based upon his experience gained at the execution grounds.
They were:—

Neck, front, side and back
Upper and lower chest
Upper and lower back
Area below the breastbone (Sternum)
Underneath floating ribs.

The vulnerability of the wrist, as a means of either disabling, or killing albeit slowly, was fully recognised fairly late on, in fact Tenshin Shoden Katori Shinto Ryu list it as one of their "Secret" techniques, along with cutting the thumb on the sword arm. The Armourers tried, rather unsuccessfully to my mind, to protect the wrist, and I include some illustrations of a number of styles, most notably

Tsutsu-Gote
Shino-Gote
Oda-Gote

In my opinion the Tsutsu Gote (Iron Wrap around) was a rather inflexible form, I have a worn a pair, during a Shrine festival, and I can attest to the fact that they make rapid movements difficult, to say the least. The preferred form, which I have worn without difficulty for the Parade of a Thousand, which is held to commemorate the death in 1617 of Tokugawa Ieyasu. This marvellous spectacle of mounted and armoured Samurai warriors takes place annually in May at the Toshogu Shrine at Nikko. My favoured style is the chain-mail Oda-Gote, as I have already stated, this form is quite comfortable for prolonged wear. As to the Shino-Gote, I have only examined a pair at my friend Mr Suzuki's House, though I hope to wear them at the next Parade of a Thousand. I will keep notes of the event, and let you know my findings.

Tsutsu-Gote

Shino-Gote

Oda-Gote

I have one last item which may be of importance, it is the item known as the 'horo', this was a cane framework, covered with material, the entire affair was strapped to a Samurai's back, so that as he rode, the wind would fill it, acting as a protective air bag against arrows. One noted writer has observed that if the Samurai maxim "Always forward, never backward" is to be believed and that Samurai never turned their backs on the enemy, how then is the horo of any use? Well, my answer, based upon what we know of the Ninja and their infiltration into Samurai armies, is simple:— A Samurai needed a horo in case any of his own side, who were Ninja in disguise, decided to shoot him in the back, taking into consideration the relative weakness against arrows, of the Japanese armour. The only exception to this is of course, the musket proof Yukinoshita-Do, which is illustrated.

In concluding this chapter, it may be considered repetition, but I feel I must say it again . . . . feudal Tameshigiri and modern Tameshigiri are not the same, although they both stress the execution of perfect "Kihaku" (release of spirit by cutting). The antique form has no place in modern society, but the modern form contributes to modern society, I urge you to research this well.

The Horo arrow catcher

6. PREPARATION FOR PRACTICE

It is no coincidence that the first five chapters of this book are taken up with the spirit of the sword, and spiritual matters, that is because, as the warriors of Satsuma Province were fond of saying "There is no strength in the strongest sword arm, if the heart is not pure". I trust you agree with this admirable sentiment, and based upon it I shall continue in the manner described by my own Master.

In the study of the sword arts, whatever the persuasion, form is important to be sure, but Genki (Vigour) is more important. It is a fact that persons who have not tested themselves by cutting a fixed object (in the modern form Tameshigiri – see Mr Obata's work on the subject) cannot hope to know what real sword-work is. It is the same as asking a blind man to describe a sunset, he can describe what people have told him a sunset looks like, but it is always going to be shallow repetition. It is felt that much of modern Budo is in this sorry state.

So, how can the sincere student counter this problem? First of all by training the inner man, by the practices explained in chapter three, notably Jigotai and the seated meditation, this must be done regularly to be of any use, it is very shallow thinking to merely try it out for a week, then dismiss it. Remember, warriors died to give these secrets to future generations, we must not allow their legacy to die out, in a way it is our link with the Ninja and the Samurai, as real now as it was when it was experienced by them. It has been described as the only tangible link with the hearts and minds of the feudal warrior, and I must agree with it.

To quell the demons of indecision and weak will; it is necessary to strengthen the body. The best way that I know, is the way the old Samurai and Ninja masters used. Simply speaking, if you use a sword weighing two and one half pounds, then practice with an iron club (Tetsu Keibo or Tetsu-To) weighing twenty pounds or slightly less, if you are unaccustomed to heavy training.

Tetsu-To

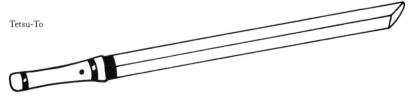

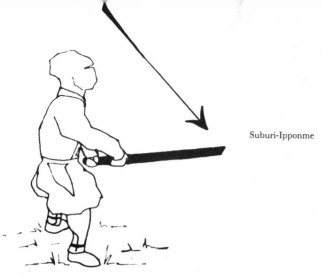

Suburi-Ipponme

TRAINING METHOD NUMBER ONE *(Suburi-Ipponme)*

Hold the tetsu-to in the carry ready position.

Stand in shizentai, breathing slowly.

Raise the tetsu-to to chudan no kamae, holding with two hands.

Raise the tetsu-to above the head, to jodan no kamae.

Invigorate your lower abdomen (tighten it slightly).

Bring down the tetsu-to forcefully to chudan level, at the same time move into ichimonji jigotai. Emit the kial shout, with the sound "Yah!"

The following practice is based upon the principal of Ki-Ken-Tai-Ichi, that is to say spirit, sword and body arrive at the same time. Thus is practice unified with spirit.

As to the amount of times you practice this most basic of all suburi, is up to you, Master Tesshu thought nothing of practicing ten thousand suburi with his "Demon Queller" (Tesshu Yamaoka, the famous warrior of the restoration period — 1868). It made Tesshu a man of resolute nature, and irresistible in battle.

There is a song that the warriors of the Ashikaga used to sing whilst practicing suburi:—

> *Swinging my club in unison*
> *I count the numbers down*
> *Was it ten or a thousand?*
> *No matter naught — just swing*
> *Today is today, and tomorrow*
> *never comes.*

Suburi-Nihonme

TRAINING METHOD NUMBER TWO *(Suburi Nihonme)*

You may start as before from shizentai, or continue from the first suburi, in ichimonji jigotai.

Step into jigotai, assuming chudan no kamae. Holding the tetsu-to in both hands raise the tetsu-to up to hidari jodan, then without pausing swing the tetsu-to in a horizontal arc above your head, moving to the left, and bringing the tetsu-to to an abrupt stop directly in front of you. Pull back the tetsu-to to migi-jodan and repeat the action, this time swinging the horizontal arc to the right, stopping abruptly in front of you.

Repeat until exhausted, then "ten more" is what my Master used to say. Of course you must be careful, and it is vital that you ask your physician before attempting these drills. Whilst they may seem simple, it is the repetition, and the affect they have upon your supplies of Ki (internal energy). It is possible to suffer from an abundance of Ki. Which gives me the opportunity to say a little about Ki. In my understanding of it, Ki is not a miraculous power, it is really quite normal, we all have it. In some of us it is stagnant, and in others it bubbles forth, how often have you seen some person who seems to turn anything he or she touches into success. This is merely Ki exerting itself as it should. Today, when many people search in vain for instant answers to their problems, it is easy to see the naturalness of Ki exerting itself as something almost mystical. It is not! The teachings of the Kurama Hachi-Ryu contain the self same methods as you will find in this book, although over eight hundred years separate them. It saddens me when I see persons who are really only strongarms using their strength to perform simple tricks, to fool gullible people; it is a shameful thing.

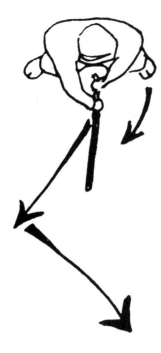

Suburi-Sanbonme
(viewed from above)

TRAINING METHOD NUMBER THREE *(Suburi Sanbonme)*
Stand in shizentai, holding tetsu-to in both hands, at chudan no kamae.

Raise the tetsu-to above your head.

Step first obliquely into right jigotai, executing the cut and kiai, as before, it is important to perform with Ki-Ken-Tai-Ichi feeling, retrieve back into shizentai.

Repeat, this time travelling forward into left jigotai, cutting as before with the tetsu-to.

Continue alternative sides with full kiai; it is important not to strain the spirit when you perform this. By straining the spirit, my Master meant to exert yourself beyond your capabilities, a literal "Surfeit of Ki" this may result in shaking hands or arms, hot and cold flushes, even loss of consciousness. A classic example of too much of a good thing. So build up slowly but surely, and remember that there is no magic about the reality of Ki. It is as simple as breathing . . . . I urge you to strive to realise it.

TRAINING METHOD NUMBER FOUR *(Suburi Shihonme)*

This is sometimes known as "Tombo Suburi" (Dragonfly Suburi) due to the shape that is described by the tetsu-to. Others have called it "figure of eight". I think that will be the best way of remembering it. Stand in ichimonji jigotai with the tetsu-to held at chudan no kamae. Start to swing the tetsu-to high up to the right, turning it at the top of the swing and returning it down to the left, so as to describe the shape of the figure eight on its side.

Important: do not use the strength of the shoulders only, the swing must start at the lower abdomen, and then extend outwards into the arms. This is a little difficult to explain in words, you must practice it to get the feeling.

71

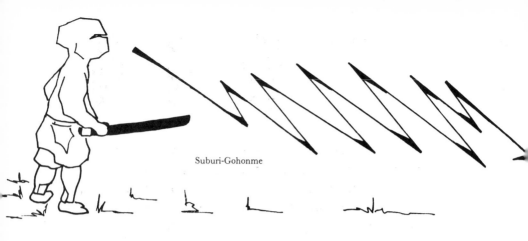

Suburi-Gohonme

TRAINING METHOD NUMBER FIVE *(Suburi Gohonme)*

This is the dreaded "ten step cutting" – I say "dreaded" humourously, because this method is most taxing, and my master used to end a session of training with it, so it was the hardest of all practice.

Start off in right oblique jigotai raise the tetsu-to and cut as you move forward into left oblique jigotai.

The action is; left, right, left, right, cutting with each forward step, when you have travelled forwards ten steps (or however many your training hall allows, due to size of training class or size of building).

Next, step back into left and right oblique jigotai cutting with the tetsu-to as the back foot lands.

With this practice, the idea is to continue, no matter what, that is the "Hell" of ten step cutting, just persevere.

You may be interested to know what type of thing can be used to construct a tetsu-to, there are a few examples of the "antique" forms of cast-iron tetsu-to; these are safe, provided they are not struck against an object, as is the nature of cast-iron to shatter like so much pottery upon impact with a hard surface. There are the rare instances of an O-Dachi form sword blade, mounted up in a large style white wood 'tsuka' (handle) bound with iron bands. Those of you who follow Aiki-do may peruse some of the older pictures of Master Uyeshiba, in the tokonoma of the room depicted, is a huge tetsu-to.

I have seen this similar form in many classical dojo; I must confess that I have no idea who made it, or even if they were all made by the same artisan. It would certainly be an unusual item to make, I am reasonably sure that they are not tempered (The O-Dachi Forms), so it

is a possibility that they were made up by the sort of smith who produced kitchen knives or door hinges for large gatehouses.

I am afraid that those of you who are reading this outside of Japan,
must as always, use your initiative. I am told of a keen student who took
his wooden suburi-to along to the local iron foundry to have a sand
mould made, and the resultant piece cast in cast iron. This shows a
great deal of enterprise, and I wish him every success. He has asked me
not to mention his name, but if I were to say that his wrists are like tree
trunks and he comes from Grand Canyon country, then those of you
who know him will recognise to whom I refer . . . .

As a last resort the type of steel stock that is used for weight training
bars may be of use, if it is not too long, and is firmly bound at the end
that is to be the handle. Circular bars have a tendency to jump, when
the hands become sweaty, that is why traditionally sword handles are
elliptical in shape. The major criticism against the tetsu-to is that it can
create a stacatto movement, which is of course amplified when one
returns to the normal sword weight. I take this criticism quite seriously,
and after several "sake discussions" with my friends in the various
classical ryu, it was felt that the logical way to eradicate this possible
over-emphasis, was to resort to the "tetsu-yari" (Iron Spear).

The techniques of the Tetsu-Yari are quite simple circling and
thrusting actions; it is important to ensure that the turning comes from
the lower abdomen, and as such is the expression of 'hara', or 'tanden'.

The tetsu-yari is simply a rod of iron about six shaku in length
(6 feet plus) though in exceptional cases a longer length is permissible.
In the ideal tetsu yari, it tapers from a diameter of approximately one
and one half inches to one inch over the length.

Tetsu-Yari

Old style Tetsu-To

Suburi Ropponme

TRAINING METHOD NUMBER SIX *(Suburi Ropponme)*
Stand in shizentai, with the tetsu-yari held taper down in the right hand.
Raise the left hand and at the same time raise the right hand, turn the
yari, the weight will take over and the yari will start to spin around,
allow it to spin in one half arc before reaching your outstretched left
arm, touch-catch the yari (i.e. don't grab it!) and allow it to continue in
its movement, guiding it down to the left side, with the taper pointing
down.
Repeat the technique, passing the yari back into the right hand.
Unlike the techniques of the tetsu-to, in which the kiai is an abrupt
"Yah". In the techniques of the tetsu-yari the kiai is a long sonorous
tone, something like "YaaaaaaaaaaaaaaaaaaaaaaaaRuuuuuuuuuuuuu-
uuuuuuuuuuuuuuuuSaaaaaaaaaaaaaaaaaaaa". It should take the entire
cycle of the breath out, as much as twenty five seconds. It should be a
deep tone.
Remember *"What was done yesterday, is the victory of today,*
　　　　　　Thus is shown the virtue of practice".
　　　　　　To paraphrase the Hozoin Spear school of the late
　　　　　　Sixteenth century.

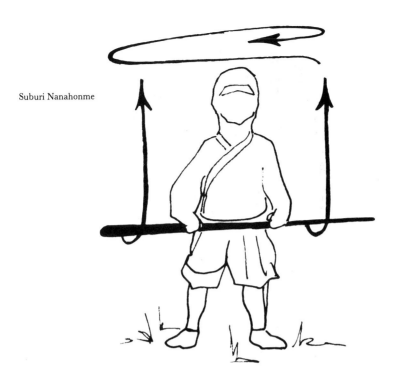

Suburi Nanahonme

TRAINING METHOD NUMBER SEVEN *(Suburi Nanahonme)*
Sometime known as "Dai Maru" (great circle)
From ichimonji jigotai hold the tetsu-yari at waist height, with the left
and right hands at hip width. At the beginning of a breathing cycle
thrust both hands up to the fullest extension, then move the tetsu-yari
in a great horizontal circle, in an upright plane (see the illustrations,
the technique is simple once mastered). The kiai is a drawn out "Tooo-
oooooooo", as the skill increases, you may rotate faster and make the
circle smaller, but be careful as the power built up in the swing can rip
the tetsu-yari out of your hands sending it off in a dangerous curving
arc, be warned.

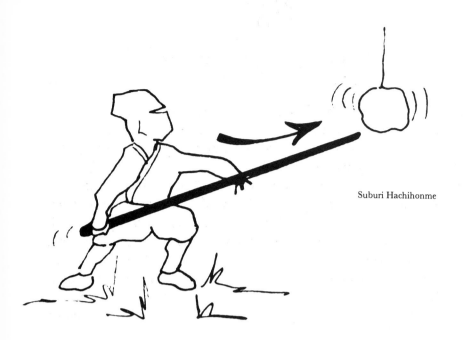

Suburi Hachihonme

TRAINING METHOD NUMBER EIGHT *(Suburi Hachihonme)*
Traditionally; suspend natural sea sponges by hempen or silk cord from the branches of a cryptomeria tree, simply thrust at them with increasing speed.

This can be done from ichimonji jigotai or from shizentai, into left or right oblique jigotai, thrusting as the front foot lands. The kiai is sharp and short — "Tak", "Yok" with a sight exhalation on the last part.

There is a variation that may be done from the eight directions movement, but it is not my preferred form, so I will mention it here in passing, suggesting that some future student will enlarge upon it.

It should be remembered that as Yamada Asaemon — grand master of the Yamada said . . . . .
"Life and Death are the same. Only the Kihaku is truth.
(Kihaku — Moment of spiritual unification during a sword cut).

7. STANCES AND GRIPS

Knowledge of true Silent Kenjutsu, must be founded upon a strong basis, in the case of a surprise attack, it was a favoured method to strike upwards from a hidden position, as the target walked unwittingly by.

There are many instances of Ninja and similar assassins digging a shallow pit at the side of the footpath, like the funnel-web spider they would wait in the pit, a light sprinkling of earth, and a few fallen branches over them; waiting to leap out with a devastating Iai-Nuki, simultaneous draw and strike. As you can imagine, rigid stances had little use in this type of covert attack. Indeed they could be the downfall of the potential master assassin. Surprise had to be total, there was a saying "Give a Samurai half a second, and he will take your head in payment" (an example of the speech of the eighteenth century Edokko merchant class).

The main stances for an effective strike were:–

> Jigotai
> Iai-Hiza
> Iai-Goshi
> Shizentai

Kenjutsu from below

JIGOTAI

As has already been stated, jigotai is singularly the most important of all the stances in what we may call true training. "A pint of sweat is a technique learned" is a saying that we would all do well to ponder.

If the intent is to cut an enemy, strongly, from the front, or from the rear, with either a cut that comes from over the head or from either of the shoulders, then jigotai is the posture to use. If you have trained sufficiently well with the tetsu-to, then this is most obvious. In the Koryu (Old school), it was necessary to master this form before any others. Indeed, Master Yamada Asaemon was reputed to be able to cut "Mitsu-Do-Setsu-Dan" or three men placed horizontally. I have seen a Sword by the famous Inoue Shinkai, which had this inscribed upon it in gold powder lacquer. I tried it out on a straw bundle, and it cut very well indeed.

The Ninja needed to spring into jigotai, quickly and easily from a number of what I could best describe as "craft positions", by this, I mean that the Ninja may pretend to be a carpenter or dyer, sake brewer or something like that, lulling his enemy into a false sense of security, then as the enemy walked past, the Ninja would draw and cut whilst dropping into whatever jigotai was necessary (ichimonji for someone walking in front, hidari or migi for someone walking towards or away from the Ninja). You must understand, that in the case of trying to strike down an important man, one who would have many Yojimbo (Bodyguards) the Ninja was virtually committing suicide; so he had to be sure that he could cut strongly and without hesitation; he had only one chance; the saying was "One Sword, one life, one cut".

Jigotai

Having made the decisive cut, the Ninja would not wish to be captured, and if escape was not possible, then he would choose death. This is very difficult for us in the twentieth century to understand, even in Japan. Let me say, first and foremost, you understand your world by what you see and fear, fear is the controlling factor in life; fear of failure, fear of death, fear of pain, fear of social inadequacy, even fear of fear itself. That is why the Budo arts are so noble, for they allow us to eradicate our fear, and "polish our heart". For a member of a Ninja group, whether it be a separate clan (in the sense of a collection of like-minded persons, not necessarily a bloodline) or as a part of a classical Ryu which contained the teachings of Ninjutsu; the feudal Ninja would have the inner strength to allow him, or her to face death resolutely, because of the belief that the style of practice was indeed Tenshin-Sho (Divinely inspired). So to die whilst performing its techniques, was in fact to become – Kami (Deity). Thus many Ninja made their vows to Amida, or Mari-shiten (Arcala), Fudo or a thousand sub deities, and bravely walked to their deaths.

IAI-HIZA

Iai-hiza, or as it is sometimes referred, tate-hiza is a difficult method to master, it involves a half sitting crouch, and relates directly to the next method of iai-goshi, which will be detailed in a moment. Now to perform correct iai-hiza I advise you to draw a figure "+" stand in shizentai in the crossing point of the two lines of the cross turn, forty five degrees to the left and squat down by bending the knees outward, but only moving on the balls of the feet, fans of kendo will recognise this as sonkyo. Facing forty five degrees to the left, now twist with the left knee, placing it on the forty five degree line as shown. Now sit down on the left heel, turning the body back to the original position direction, as you do so you must place your right foot close to your left knee, allow your right knee to relax down. This is Iai-Hiza.

It was said the Ninja were able to sit upon the prow of a boat in a storm, without moving from Iai-Hiza. I have not been able to trace the source of this story, so I will leave it only as hearsay, unless some other person can supply the exact details. In the Yama-Niwa style of mountainous garden, sometimes referred to as the "world in miniature" it was easy for a Ninja to adopt the Iai-Hiza form, and simply wait for his

 Iai-Hiza

 Iai-Goshi

 Shizentai

enemy. This I am firmly convinced is the origin of all those wild tales concerning Ninja being able to transform themselves into rocks and trees. I do know that the Mito Ninja trained in a rudimentary form of simile-association, whereby they would imagine the shape of the form which they desired to hide themselves amongst; thus it was possible to remain still and silent in a rock garden, or flow with the movement of a bamboo grove. The human eye is a fickle thing, if it believes that a thing is not out of place, then to all intents and purposes, it is not. I will give you an example of this, which was related to me by my friend from England; suppose you save all your spare money, and purchase an object, such as an automobile; for a few days, the vehicle will be perfect in your eyes, but as you become accustomed to it you will notice tiny flaws and imperfections. They were there when you bought it, but because you did not expect to see any flaws in your long awaited purchase, there were none. Do you see the point that I am making? If you do not expect a thing to be present, then your eye may well see the item, but your brain will not register it. This is the fundamental method of modern camouflage, but the feudal Ninja well understood its secrets over five centuries ago.

IAI-GOSHI

Iai-Goshi is the combat-ready stance popular to most of the feudal Ryu, as I said before, this is very close to Iai-Hiza in its form (in certain ryu the names are interchangeable). If you can adopt Iai-Hiza with ease, then Iai-Goshi will present little problem in its basic form. To adopt the basic Iai-Goshi, again using the figure "+" stand in shizen-tai, squarely. Place the left knee at forty five degrees to the left, and sit back — lightly on the left raised heel. The right foot should be just a little in front, you must experiment with this, as no two ryu agree exactly upon this, my advice is to adopt a position which is comfortable, yet strong. There is nothing worse than a person adopting a stance that is forced and stiff, correct reaction is then made impossible. In all this, the right knee is raised slightly and thirty degrees off the straight line. That is the basic form, which allows a rapid rise up, particularly useful in cutting 'gyaku kesa' style, which involves rotating the scabbard ninety degrees so that the cutting edge of the blade exits facing down; the sword then curves up in a powerful arc, usually about fifteen degrees off the vertical (its name comes from the robe of the Buddhist Priest known as 'kesa'). This move coupled with a powerful springing up results in what has been called "otoko-wari" – man-splitter.

If the sword were strapped to the back in 'gyaku ushiro' style, then the action of the draw was started only after the leap up had begun. The scabbard is pulled away from the sword in a left oblique downward direction. The sword itself being pulled up and back in a right oblique upward direction, ending up in what can best be described, rather nonsensically as "Ushiro no Kamae". Please refer to the illustrations of this most complex movement.

For an extremely complex reason this stance is referred to as "Goyemon-Hiza" by the Mito Ninja. Basically the reason is this:–

Two hundred years ago the Mito Ninja used to use a large bath tub filled with water to aid their training in iai-goshi. The student would immerse himself in the bath tub, squatting in iai-goshi, so that the water was just below his nostrils. Upon the command of his senior the student was to leap up and out of the bath tub. This of course was extremely difficult as you can imagine. For the water was acting as a resistance to the movement. However when after several weeks of this gruelling training the student attempted to perform iai-goshi outside of the tub, his leap was extremely strong. The name came about, so it is told, due to the fact that a normal all wooden bath tub would soon fall apart with the strain of hard training. The only solution to this was to use a tub which had an iron bottom. This form has traditionally been called Goyemon-Furo after the legendary robber leader Ishikawa Goyemon, who was boiled alive in one of them. Hence the rather quaint "Goyemon-Hiza".

SHIZENTAI

Normally shizentai would be dismissed by the beginner as only a starting posture, but this is wholly inaccurate. In a crowded street, the "machi-wari" street cutter technique was most effective, allowing "wayfarers" to cut down their enemy whilst avoiding an obvious aggressive stance. It must be said, that this would only work against one of the merchant classes, as no self respecting Samurai would ever allow anyone to invade what I suppose we should call "his personal space". It is interesting to note that at the okuden level (very advanced)

Various grips

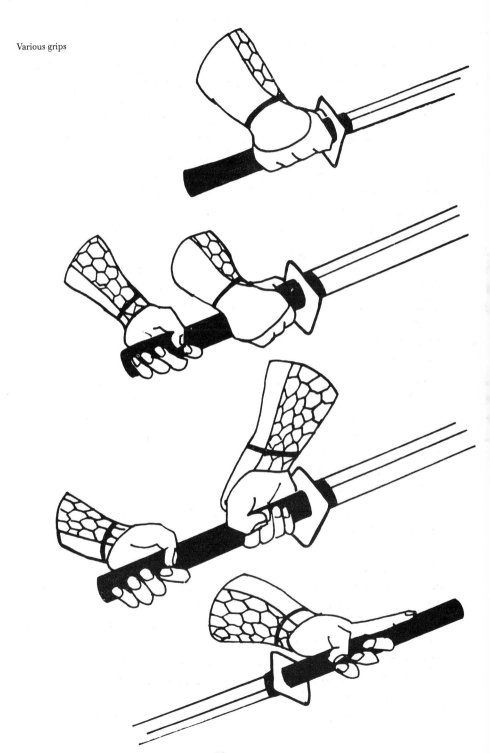

of many ryu, there is a facet of training, which can best be referred to as "single tatami" iai. That is to say that no particular stances are involved, and movement is kept to a minimum, instead relying upon the fastest of actions of cutting and sheathing. It must be said that this form is, as it were, only a killing action. It involves the resheathing of a soiled blade, an act which was inexcusable under normal circumstances, but in a crowd, such as would occur in a main street at festival time, a skilful Ninja, or apprentice "cutter down" could draw, strike and resheathe in an instant making good his escape in the crowd. Countless cases are documented by the Tokugawa Judicial system; it has even been suggested that certain unscrupulous Samurai would test out their blades against innocent bystanders in this fashion. No martial family is prepared to admit to this disgraceful behaviour in any of their ancestors, but it certainly was prevalent during the rule of Shogun Ietsugu, in 1713.

GRIPS

The needs of the Ninja swordsman was totally different to that of the Buke (samurai) swordsman, though there were certainly several similarities of the basic form. These students of iai-do will recognise as "shibori", which is the wringing out action performed with the hands, as it were into themselves. Please refer to my illustration of this, as often when I say to western students to make a wringing action, they inevitably make this in the horizontal plane as opposed to the forward plane. I am intrigued by this subtle difference in understanding. Now assuming that the correct shibori is in practice; grasp the tsuka in the normal "right hand at tsuba end and left hand at tsuka-gashira (kashira)". Let us take for example the simplest case of a cut coming from jodan no kamae, raise the sword smoothly from chudan no kamae until you can feel the muscles of the lower ribcage, on both sides, this should be a feeling of slight "pulling". If you have trained well in the tetsu-to method from jigotai, this should present little difficulty. With the blade at its fullest extension back, bring the hands forward and down. Please do not let the tip waver from its target otherwise the force and spirit of the cut will be lost (kihaku). This is vital, you must not fail in this aspect of training. As the 'mono-uchi' (area of maximum cutting effect) nears the target, strengthen your abdomen and allow the kiai to come out as the sound "Eh!" or "Toh!" This should all coincide with the wringing action of shibori. For iai-do, that is all there is to the cut, but if you wish to test your skill as the masters of old, using green bamboo or straw bundles, then as you cut you must pull the blade into yourself. I will not detail this any further, as my friend Mr. Obata covers this subject in his book, which is called "Naked Blade – A Manual of Japanese Swordsmanship". I again advise you to refer to it if you desire to improve your skill in the best way.

Gyaku-Te

Among the feudal Ninja's uses of what I term "silent kenjutsu" was a particular grip, which is singular to the clandestine nature of Ninja practice. In this the right hand is reversed in a most unorthodox manner, so that the littlest finger is closest to the tsuba (handguard). This "gyaku-te" (reverse hand) allows for a sharp cutting action to be followed by a stabbing thrust. You will notice from the illustrations of this technique, that it has a number of possible uses in clearing a narrow corridor, and as such it was used by many Ninja clans. When a diversionary action had to be made in confined spaces this allowed the maximum useful effect of both the cutting edge and the point. It also allowed the sword to be swung around, one handed to a carry-ready position, similar to a waki kamae; this was particularly useful when the enemy did not know the correct combat engagement distance, due to the length of the blade being hidden. It was a simple matter to flip the blade into a semi gyaku kesa cut, whilst moving away from the main line of the enemy's reflex attack.

There is a grip, and release, which was designed to be used with a blade below chiisa katana length (approximately eighteen inches blade length). This was rather quaintly referred to as 'tsubame-ken' (swallow tail sword). This starts from the gyaku-te grip, single handed, the blade is then slashed down and flicked away at the enemy. This was most unorthodox, most Samurai were schooled from childhood that a dropped or thrown sword was great dishonour. Thus the feudal Ninja took note of the behaviour pattern of his enemy, and exploited the areas that the enemy would not expect. Thus the Ninja was able to overcome a superior opponent, by causing "suki" that is to say a gap in the concentration.

Kiri-Te Hocho

8. OTHER WEAPONS

It was the noble Musashi Miyamoto who said "There is a right time and a right place for the use of weapons". By this, he was observing the age old fact that under certain circumstances, a particular weapon has the advantage. I bring your attention to the Battle of Nagashino, which took place on the 29th of June 1575. The forces of Takeda Katsuyori, his loyal aides, Baba Nobuhara Naito Kiyonaga and Yamagata Masakage were drawn up in front of a stream. On the other side of the stream was the most powerful army to date, in Samurai history, with no lesser generals than:— Tokugawa Ieyasu, Toyotomi Hideyoshi, Oda Nobunage and Okubo Tadayo. On the command of the Takeda the vast ranks of cavalry spurred their horses forward with the Takeda Battle cry on their lips "Fierce as the fire, strong as the wind and immoveable as the mountain" (please note there are several versions of this battle cry, I choose this one, my apologies to those who favour another). The Takeda Cavalry had crushed all that stood before them in a score of engagements, but this day was different, within seconds the pride of the Takeda had been blown apart by a murderous fusilade of the thousand or more Matchlock Teppo (guns) firing in volleys, the well trained troops dessimated the Takeda. All the leading generals lay dead, and a bloody rout ensued. It was the end of an era in battlefield warfare, one which the Western World would have to wait until the terrible carnage of the First World War to realise; that against trained riflemen, cavalry is nothing. I hope you realise the reason behind my short recreation of this old battle, because it illustrates my point quite well.

Firing the gun

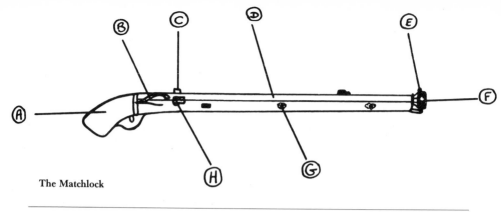

The Matchlock

A	Dai	D	Tsutsu	G	Shinogime
B	Kikan	E	Sakimeate	H	Hizara
C	Atomeate	F	Suguchi		

Thus a long sword is useless indoors, but a short sword or makura-yari (literally a pillow spear) is eminently successful in interior conflicts. A short sword can be used not only to fight, but also to literally "cut" one's way out of trouble, as occurred in 1866, when two "Shishi" (men who were opposed to foreign incursions into Japan) were attacked by a Tokugawa execution squad. The well-documented attack, was performed Ninja style at dead of night. The two Shishi, who have become the subject of many stories and motion pictures, were Sakamoto Ryoma and Miyoshi Shinzo. The two friends were travelling to nearby Kyoto, when they decided to break their journey and stay at a Ryokan (Inn) at Fushimi. The Ninja attack began, and about twenty of the Tokugawa Samurai crowded into the inn, swords

Sakamoto

Makura-Yari

drawn and spears readied. Sakamoto woke up and his friend Miyoshi reached for his sword, he had decided to "sell his life dearly", which is to say that he was prepared to stand and fight until death, but Sakamoto had important business still to do, so instead of drawing a sword, drew a Colt pistol. As the Ninja assassins burst into their upstairs room, Sakamoto fired all six shots in rapid succession, dropping a few of the would be killers. Whilst Sakamoto struggled to reload, Miyoshi held them off with his sword. The onslaught was too strong and a Ninja cut at Sakamoto's hand.

The gun fell to the floor and Sakamoto drew his short sword; briefly the two friends beat back the attack, sending bodies flying down the stairs. This was the brief respite they needed, and Sakamoto seized the initiative, using his short sword, he cut through into the next room, and so on until they came to the back of the inn. The Tokugawa assassination squad were so confident of their superiority that they neglected to post a guard at the rear of the building, and so Sakamoto and Miyoshi made good their escape, into an enclosed courtyard. Without pausing to take a second breath they calmly smashed their way through the neighbouring house, until they came to the street. The front of the inn was crowded by onlookers, so the Tokugawa did not notice their quarry make good their escape.

On the classical battlefield it was said that a man with a spear was twenty paces of advantage in a straight line, but a man with a naginata

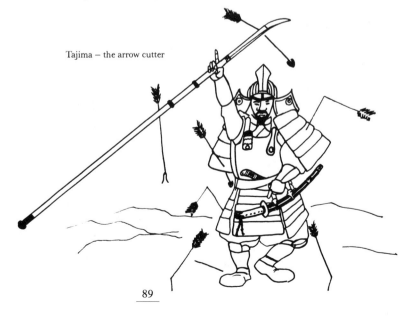

Tajima – the arrow cutter

or a nagimaki was twenty paces long by twenty paces wide advantage. That means, that whilst the spear was quick in its thrusting movement, an enemy could run alongside the spearman, rendering the spear useless. A naginata however, having a long sharp curved blade could cut a swathe in the ranks of an enemy. There is of course the occasion that is documented in the Heike Monogatari (Tales of the Heike) Tajima — the arrow cutter. Gochiin no Tajima was a warrior who was skilled with the naginata, so much so, that at the Uji bridge incident he was reputed as having stood at the front on a spar of the broken Uji bridge defying all to try to pass. As such he was a perfect target for archers, this he paid no heed, instead he cut any arrow that came close to hitting him. I must confess to being of the opinion that he was lucky. I will not detail the use of naginata and nagamaki, in great detail, for to truly do these excellent weapons justice would take a separate volume apiece.

Sode Gaki and Sode Garami in use.

90

NAGINATA

The naginata is a decendant of the ancient "Hoko", which in the records of the time, date it as being used during the reign of Shomu-Tenno (Emperor of all Japan 724-749). The Hoko was a straight bladed stabbing spear, secured to spear shaft by a socket fitting. As time progressed, the weakness of this system demanded that the tang should be made similarly to the sword, and the shaft hollowed out to accommodate it. This bound around with copper or iron bands, produced a much stronger weapon, allowing really forceful thrusting actions to be made. Here in the development of polearms, the paths go their separate ways, on the one hand the yari spear form, and on the other, the naginata.

The naginata came about as a result of the experiments made with the Hoko, as I have already said, this strong weapon became the scourge of the battlefield, and there are reports that especially strong blades were capable of cutting the legs of a cavalry horse off, in mid gallop.

The nagimaki was a compromise weapon, being a shaft slightly shorter than the naginata, into this a full length sword blade was placed.

It would be imperative that a Ninja be aware of the fighting method used in naginata-jutsu, and as such most recorded ryu placed great emphasis upon naginata from Kamakura times (1192 until 1336), though it was relegated to principally a "house defensive" weapon during the Tokugawa reign (1600-1868), becoming lighter in weight and slighter in design. It is now popular as a woman's sport which is a recent development.

SODE-GAKI

Literally "sleeve" entanglers were the item of restraint used by Police forces and firefighters, they were really strangely shaped poles, with a profusion of barbs and spikes which would catch upon a person, rendering them incapable of wielding a sword effectively. These were always kept in the gate-houses of Japanese castle towns, and were the only way of restraining a warrior who had had too much to drink . . . .

YUMI

The bow, is synonymous with the Samurai, almost as much as the sword, and great emphasis was placed upon acquiring skill with it. In the great cavalry exchanges of the thirteenth century the classical assymetrical bow (see illustration) was used from horseback in the style known as yabusame. The giant warrior Tametomo was alleged to have used a bow which was almost nine shaku long (note one shaku equals approximately 11.93 inches), though six shaku and five sun (approximately six feet five inches) is the normal length. The bow is traditionally made up of strips of bamboo and 'haze' (a sinuous wood) glued together and bound with twine made from hempen cord, or rattan cane. There were half bows, designed for short range work, and socketed folding bows for Ninja type operations, the latter of course would be of crude manufacture and even wilder accuracy. The standard length bow was said to be equal to the gun in terms of range and accuracy. There are those (mostly archers) who say that in the skilled hands of a master archer, the bow was superior to all forms of weapon, on and off the battle field. To the Ninja, it was not used greatly as a method of assassination, due to the possibility of using "Kagemusha", decoy warriors, who at long distance would look like the Lord who's life was threatened. There is a saying amongst the Mito Ninja, that the only test of a true Ninja is that of the steel-length (sword length) in killing.

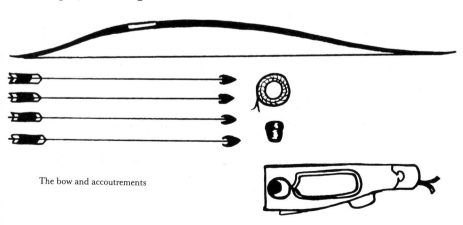

The bow and accoutrements

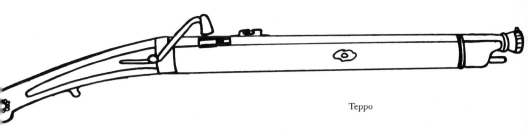

Teppo

TEPPO

The gun was the latecomer in the history of armed conflict, although the Japanese are recorded to have used rockets of Chinese design as far back as the thirteenth century, cannon were never really investigated as items of practical war use, and as such few examples remain of any totally Japanese design or manufacture. Ninja however, used the explosive powders considerably. In the first cases, for sending intelligence messages a long distance, possibly into a besieged castle or from a boat. Many of these "fire tubes" were hollowed out tree trunks bound around with rough iron strappings, they were in reality more dangerous to the owners than the targets.

The first accurate guns came from half a world away, on board a Portuguese trader warship, it landed in western Japan, on an island which has become a name for firearms . . . . . Tanegashima. The first weapons to land, in 1543 were matchlocks, interest in these items was great and a mere twenty years later no self respecting War-Lord was without his troop of musket-men. Famous workers in iron, even swordsmiths, turned their attention to the production of matchlocks, and the design remained pretty much the same until the arrival of percussion and pinfire in the nineteenth century.

It is recorded that the swordsmith Hankei made Teppo (guns) under the special art-name of Kiyotaka. So excellent were his guns that the Tokugawa ordered fifteen to be made between the years 1610 and 1615, these were strangely for the times, offered as temple gifts all over Japan, the reason for this is a mystery.

The renowned tsuba maker (sword-guard) from Higo province, Hayashi Matashichi also produced fine guns, I have fired one of these at a traditional arts meeting, and can attest to their noise, if not their accuracy. It is becoming an item of some interest these days, amongst those who revere our past.

HI-YA

These were fire arrows, I have deliberately separated them from archery, for they owe more to the skills of the gunner than the bowman, indeed Samurai bowmen would not allow a hi-ya to be fired from a good bow. This ban was bound up with the Heigaku (martial science). More of this in chapter nine.

HIYA-ZUTSU

These were rudimentary light cannon, they were originally designed as fire tubes for larger fire arrows, but several experimenters found them useful for laying caltrops (spikes to stop pursuit) over a large area. As a smashing-down weapon, they were of little use, lacking in blast strength.

KAKAE-ZUTSU

The hand cannon was usually a well made, if useless item, it was popular for Daimyo to have a pair at the back of a great parade, to dissuade any sneak attack, though their effectiveness has never been put to the test.

TANJU

Pistols in Japan were a haphazard affair, being in design and execution little more than cut down versions of the Bajo-Zutsu matchlock gun. There are examples of multi-barrel version, but these are more for the leisure-time Samurai, than the real warrior. I have even seen a twenty barrel Tanju, but this was so over detailed as to be more a work of art, than a work of war. Guns were made in three separate and distinct styles, 'kunitomo', 'tanegashima' and 'sakai', the names come from the places where they were chiefly made.

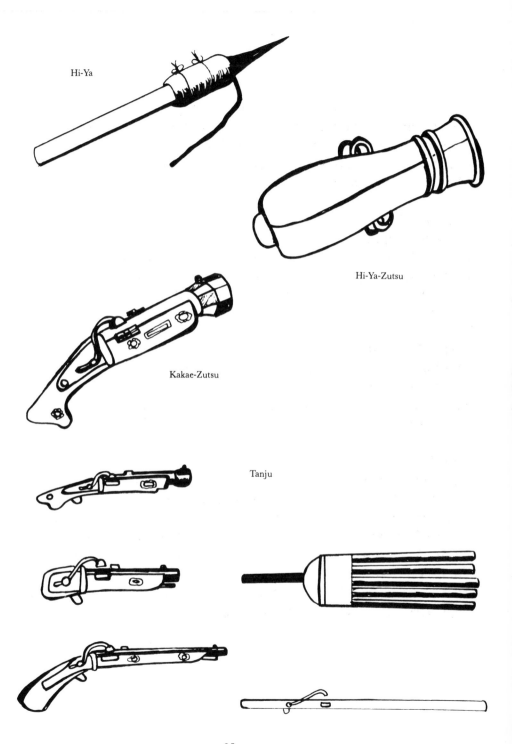

Hi-Ya

Hi-Ya-Zutsu

Kakae-Zutsu

Tanju

9. CONTROLLING THE HEART

The inner calm, that was the heart of silent Kenjutsu, had many names, given by men who knew little of philosophy, or for that matter any other conceptual form of belief. What they did know, was that their environment was their own teacher; often a term has come into use as a direct result of some personal experience within the heart of nature. Often these mind controllers (heart) studies have names which liken the experience to the nature of willow (yanagi) bamboo (take) and the direct observation of natural phenomena upon them. The elemental forces of wind, rain, snow and heat; occur frequently in the research material available.

"The willow bends in the wind, yet does not break" is one of the most popular observations of natural phenomena. The classical warrior was often heard to quietly say this before attempting an important task. Equally when all the odds were against a warrior, and seemingly no way out was possible, the saying had the effect of "controlling the heart" sufficiently for, an escape to be made, or a worthwhile death to be achieved.

"The bamboo bears the weight of winter snow, then all at once discards it as it were a coat, to stand once more proud." This is the observation of bamboo, under a seemingly impossible weight of snow in winter, the strain is taken, and the snow falls off, without harming the bamboo at all. This was seen to demonstrate the Samurai virtue of enduring that which it was normally not possible to endure.

One of the most intriguing studies in "controlling the heart" was the study of Iro-no-Kami . . . . The study of divine colours. If the person wore colours which were auspicious then in any endeavour he could not fail, thus the belief came about that the following, was real power:—

> Wood
> Fire
> Earth
> Metal
> Water

Ki – Wood

Hi – Fire

Tsuchi – Earth

Kane – Metal

Midzu – Water

Now it was believed that Wood was born from Water, and the colour of water was black; thus a person wearing black, in the place that he called his "Centre" allied all the elements to himself, for wood was opposite to water in its coded occurrence.

Earth is born of Fire, and the colour of fire is red, thus those who place their nature in the great earth spirit, should wear red.

Metal comes from earth and fire, and the colour of metal is Blue, because the elements so co-joined come to their strength by the tempering, which is always done in water, thus is the circle completed.

Such matters were thought to be auspicious (sosei).

There was a whole art to creating inauspicious effects, similar to the West African forms of Ju-Ju and the Carribbean Voodoo. Let me say that these "sokoku" practices were the result of the natural superstitious nature of feudal times; they have no use today. However if a warrior felt that he was the victim of a sokoku attack, he had recourse to the use of "takuboku", that is to say the "woodpecker", this is quite difficult to understand, but simply it means that the multicoloured woodpecker neutralised all inauspicious colours. It is no coincidence that the edge lacing on Japanese armour, is known as takuboku-ito, precisely for its calming properties.

I am often asked why the colour white occurs on sword mounts, notably the Ito-maki braid on the tsuka (handle). It is the general popular opinion that this is a reference to those warriors who had a "death-wish", or were engaged in a hopeless task; the colour of mourning and death is white in Japan, not black as is popular in the West.

Such auspicious colours were believed to be the secrets of the great clans, this of course was prevalent in the period of great battles. This was known by later researchers as "Shisei-no Yoroi".

Menuki in form of Naginata and scroll

Sword guard in the form
of a willow tree after
Kyō-Sukashi

Sword guard in the form
of bamboo – after Tadamsa
of the Akasaka

SHISEI-NO-YOROI:–   YELLOW for the great clan TACHIBANA

PURPLE for the great clan TAIRA

GREEN for the great clan FUJIWARA

BLACK for the great clan MINAMOTO

In the study of the controlled heart, there were certain numbers and combinations of numbers, that the classical warrior would use to control himself in times of great stress, for example before a battle or a duel. One such group of numbers which a follower of Kwannon would recite was the:–

SAIKOKU SANJUSAN-SHO

This was really a list of places that were sacred to Kwannon, in and around the old capitol of Kyoto, the belief being, that reciting the names of the places in full, would give the warrior the help of all the faithful who burned incence, rang the bell, or clapped their hands together in prayer before the Shrine.

To perform Saikoku Sanjusan-Sho, stand in shizentai, like the hands and fingers together in a knot like grip, and swiftly chant the following:–

"Nachi-San, Ki Miidera, Kokawa-dera, Makino-dera, Fujii-dera,
Tsubosaka-dera, Oka-dera, Nanyen-do, Mimuroto-dera, Kami-daigo-dera,
Iwama-dera, Ishiyama-dera, Mii-dera, Imagumano, Kiyomidzu-dera,
Rokuhara-dera, Rokkaku-do, Ko-do, Yoshimine-dera, Ano-ji, Soji-ji,
Katsuo-dera, Nakayama-dera, Shin Kiyomidzu-dera, Hokke-zan,
Shosha-zan, Narial-ji, Matsuno-o-dera, Chikubu-ji, Chomei-ji,
Kwannon-ji, Tanigumi-dera . . . . ."

That would be repeated many times, with increasing speed, until the sound became almost a monotone. It should be noted that this form of practice fell out of favour with most warriors in the "easier" days of the

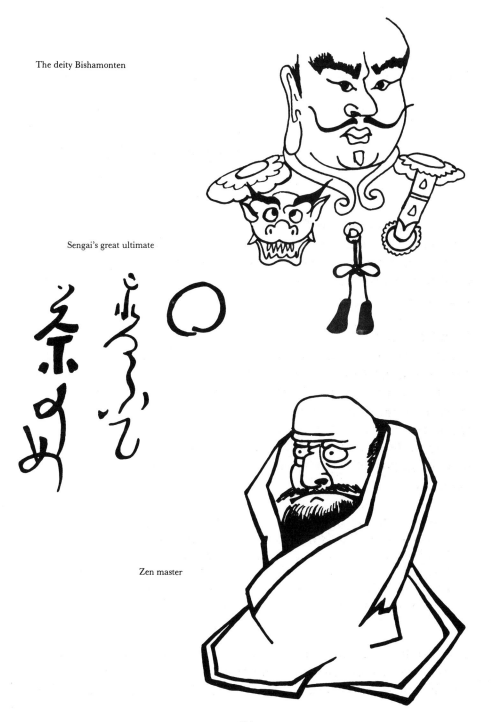

The deity Bishamonten

Sengai's great ultimate

Zen master

Tokugawa rule. I include it here as a charming link with a long vanished feudal era.

Far simpler number combinations existed of course, ones that were not such a drain upon the memory, let us start simply by the repetition of a particular Deity's name; this would be repeated and repeated until it again became a monotone, the reasoning behind this was to create a state of mindlessness, or as has become popular with modern martial artists "The mind of no-mind".

The Deities were –   Yebisu
Daikokuten
Fukurokuju
Hoteiosho
Bishamonten
Benzaiten
Jurojin

The sworde blade had many hiding places

In later years this became merely a recipe for "Good Luck".

There was also the "Understanding of Five", this was a vast study, but as with all these methods; it served to calm the mind.

Five was traditionally the celestial number, all objects came from the "Go-Gio" (Five Elements)

The Go-Gio – KI_____Wood
HI_____Fire
TSUCHI_____Earth
KANE_____Metal
MIDZU_____Water

Which, as we have already discussed were linked to the theory of Colours. This was known as "Go-Shiki" (Five Colours).

Go-Shiki – SEI_____Blue
O_____Yellow
SEKI_____Red
BIAKU_____White
KOKU_____Black

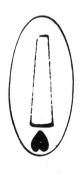

The ornamental Seppa

You will note that the names are the ancient elemental namings, not the modern; Blue – Aoi, Yellow – Kiiroi, Red – Akai, White – Shiroi, Black – Kuroi.

Amongst the elemental forces of creation were the metals. The ancients believed there were five, and these five valued as being "balanced", though how this was accomplished, I do not know, they were known as Go-Kin (Five Metals).

Go-Kin –   KIN_____Gold (Yellow)
                         GIN_____Silver (White)
                         DO_____Red (Copper)
                         TETSU_____Iron (Black)
                         SUZU_____Tin (Blue)

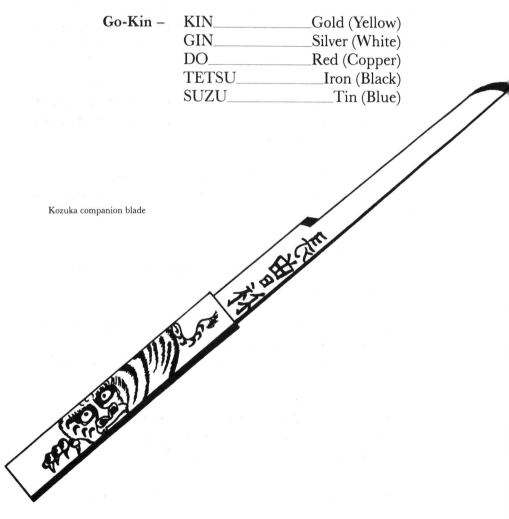

Kozuka companion blade

It is always a matter of some confusion, particularly upon the first sight of the colours, typically they seem to be out of sequence, but this is due to the fact that the various ryu may term a certain colour as having a particular relevance, which another ryu would discount. It is therefore a matter of choice, I regret that there is not enough space here to fulfill the complete listing, which would of necessity take up the latter part of this book.

There was amongst the warriors of the Nabeshima Han in the old province of Hizen, on the Island of Kyushu in Southern Japan, a practice for "controlling the heart" known as "Hamanomezarashi" (sea-sand vision), which was in reality a form of Zen type koan. A koan was traditionally a question that demanded an answer beyond normal senses; in other words, it was something that could not be grasped by the conscious mind, thus was the heart controlled. Some famous koans that have been used by warriors are:−

1 *"Say plainly what is the bucket without a bottom."*
(A reference to the illusion of reflections in water, and how much of what we perceive as "life" is but an illusion.)

2 *"How is it when you meet the dragon?"*
(A reference to what one perceives as real, and what one wishes were real.)

3 *"How do you bear out the sixteen foot image of Jizo through the eight foot door of Kenchoji?"*
(A reference to the accomplishment of the impossible against great odds.)

4 *"Here is the sound of two hands clapping;*
What now is the sound of one hand clapping?"
(The question seems insoluble, but is it?)

To be blunt, the methods so far described were and are, merely desen-

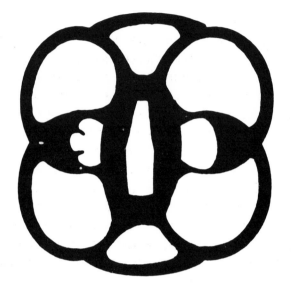

Owari sword guard

Sword guard in form
of drying nets

sitizing excercises, that is to say that they are designed to create a reality that is not as it were "head orientated". By this, you must understand that the practice opens up the subconscious channels to the very heart of nature. It is in a sense, a means of returning to one's own true nature. In this state, all things are viewed coldly, dispassionately. In the case of an attack, it is parried with unfailing accuracy, it may be said that the cultivation of this so-called "controled heart" is the very gateway to the root of existence. There is no difference therefore between life and death, good and evil, all things are subjective, existing only in the moment that is the eternal "Now". What has not yet been, may never be, and what has been is gone, as useless as if it were never in existence. This is the very core of the spirit that can create the "Zetsumyo Ken" — Miracle working sword. We must all try to be worthy of its spirit. But if we do not practice, how can we succeed?

Fuchi Kashira in form
of lightning bolts

Fuchi Kashira in form
of cobwebs

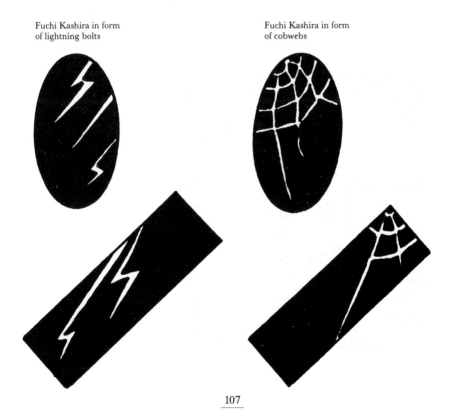

10. SPECIAL DRILLS AND "SECRET WAYS"

Let us understand that the relationship between the perfect cut and the perfect timing, is the realisation of perfect control of the heart. This trinity can only be brought about by rigorous training. I suggest a number of methods, which may be of some slight help, coming as they do from a cross-section of the ryu.

The forest run, is a technique that has favour amongst the ryu of the Northern side of the great Nakasendo road, its wooded way ran all the way to Edo (present day Tokyo) from Kyoto, through the mountainous and (in those days) heavily forested provinces of Omi, Mino, Shinano, Kai and Musashi. The practice was simply to select a running pace and once begun, not to falter or alter the speed; it need not be fast, about five miles an hour over rough ground is adequate. Just keep running up and over fallen logs dodging and weaving as the pathway becomes blocked. Do not be afraid to double back if the way ahead becomes blocked; the purpose of the exercise is to continue, you must research this sufficiently well.

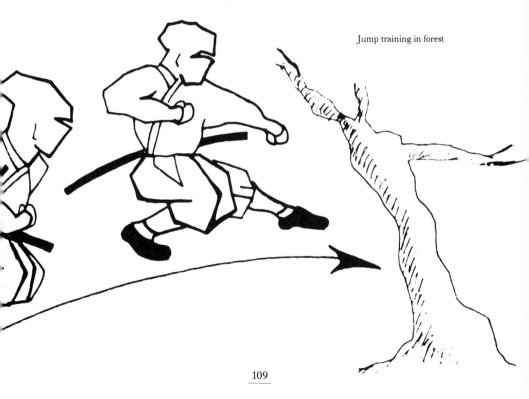

Jump training in forest

Make no mistake, as with the warrior of old, there is no second chance. Some may regard this a secret, and so it was amongst a certain class, and at an uncertain time; if you desire to make that degree of skill which the Ninja possessed, your own; you must grasp the challenge firmly, without shrinking away. Remember there are many who start, but few who finish, and that is the greatest sadness of all.

Using the forest as your training partner and master again, I suggest the following drill; as the purpose of this book is to discuss Silent Kenjutsu and the arts of the true sword, all the training will be carried out with the sword or tetsu-to. There is a group of practices the overall name of which, is "falling". The idea being to practice Nuki-uchi simultaneous draw and cut, the forest will allow this in a number of ways. In Autumn it is the leaf falling from the tree, as the tree prepares for Winter, spiritually it is the karma of the leaf to fall, and if your heart is pure, it is the karma of the blade to meet with and cut the leaf.

In Winter, when the trees are heavy with snow, just walk, slowly, centering your spirit, when some snow falls at its right time (as the

Swordsman Yamagata termed it) your sword will draw itself and cut as if you were a bystander. In the Spring it will be the blossom that will test your resolve, and in the Summer you may cut at the Summer rains.

Ninja forest run

This sort of practice, deep within nature, is something that many of the greatest warriors have indulged in but be warned, many have died practicing it.

I do not say this lightly, for nature is boundless, and will not be fooled with !!!!!!!. You must be pure in your resolve to create true Budo. By this I mean that you must strive deeply and honestly to know whether a technique works; and if it does not, then you must have the honesty to admit your error and start all over again. Think seriously about this, there are many men in the world today who hide behind their shortcomings.

"If the forest cannot teach you its secrets, then how can you progress"? That is a paradox that was considered as a secret teaching by the warriors of the Mito Ninja. Now what does it mean, and how can it have any relevance to us today?

The answer to this is both simple and profound; for the forest, substitute natural order, or whatever it is that you call sacred. For progress, you can substitute realisation. This is simply to say you must not try to impose values upon that which is beyond value. And that is the truest progress that any feeling human being can make. It is just a sword, that

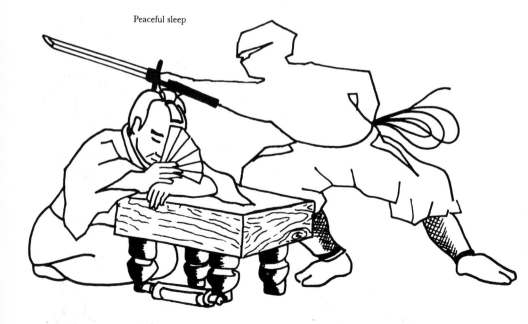

Peaceful sleep

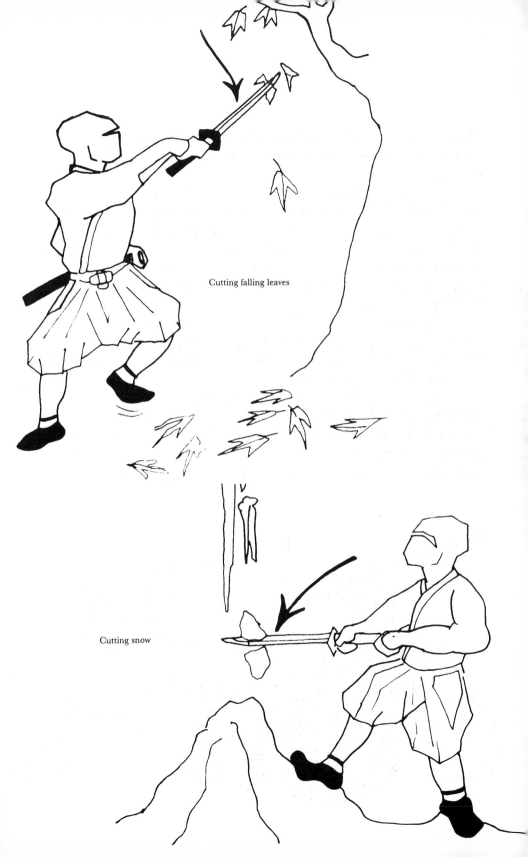

Cutting falling leaves

Cutting snow

comes between man and nature. That is a deep concept to understand; basically you must be natural in your action, if you can point from one position to another smoothly without a weapon, why cannot you do it with a weapon in your hand? Why is it that when we have a thing to do, which is in someway considered to be "manly". The movements of the body become stiff and erratic? I will leave the answer to be found by you yourself, in whatever way you think fit.

The early morning is a test in itself, "I challenge the day", was a popular saying amongst the Tosa warriors. That is to say, the morning practice, over the years is the most telling practice. If it is conducted alone, then the tests it imposes are the truest victories, and the most painful of failures. You must persevere, not only in this, but in all aspects of your life, pay attention to the smallest of details, for they are important. It was said that the real test of a warrior, was not how he conducted himself in the weighty affairs of state, but how how he lifted his tea-cup; it reveals a great deal about the inner strength of a warrior, for in the little things, one is unguarded.

So let us consider some special drills, I make no distinction as to the choice of weapon in these drills, it is perfectly acceptable to use either katana, with a curved blade, or the straight musori blade, so popular in the cinema. It is up to you to chose your weapon, of course if

Fuchi-Kashira in form of bamboo

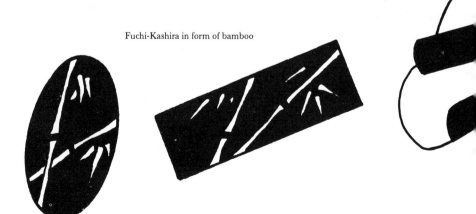

114

you are usng what I would call a "live" blade, that is to say, one that has a sharpened edge absolute safety is important, I draw your attention to the rules for safe practice, which appear in "The Ninja Star — Art of Shurikenjutsu". For those of you who do not have access to a copy, let me condense them, with particular attention to Sword work.

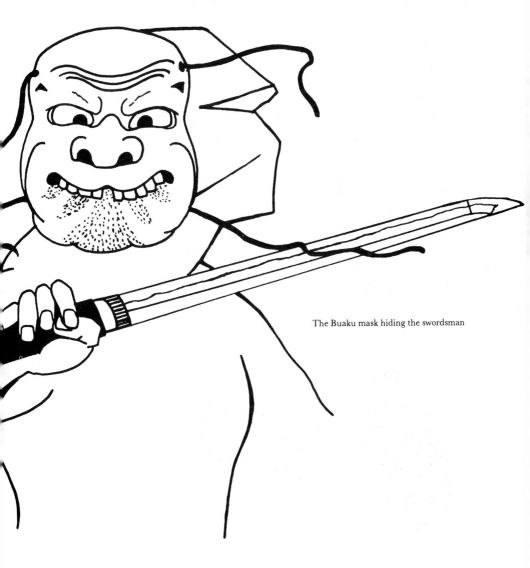

The Buaku mask hiding the swordsman

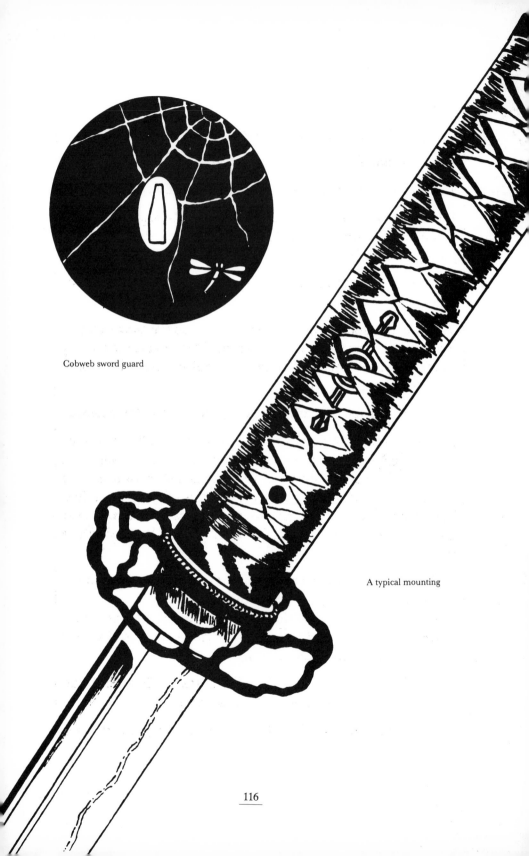

Cobweb sword guard

A typical mounting

1 Check that Sword is in good condition.

2 Check that all fixing pins are sound.

3 Check that handle bindings are in good condition.

4 Check that the scabbard is sound (in practicing with a "live" blade, it is possible to cut through the scabbard; severely injuring the hand).

5 Check your training space (this is vital, if in doubt, do not practice).

6 Do not transport your weapon to and from the place of training in such a way that it can be drawn. The best advice is carry your sword in a closed cloth bag in a lockable case, always carry your affiliation card with you.

7 Never brag about your sword skill, and offer to demonstrate.

8 Arguments about who would win in an all out attack between a swordsman and a Karate-ka, Judo-ka, are both stupid and dangerous; you must understand that there is no comparison to be made, for the only ending of a sword conflict, is in death of either or both parties. Please be of no doubt, that the reality of a sword duel is in death, and a bloody death at that.

9 If you see a person practicing in a dangerous manner with a sword, it is your duty to correct this error.
(By this, I do not mean that you must intervene and cause trouble, you must change the opinion due to practice by your own example. This is very important.)

10 Lastly but in premier order of importance; if in doubt do not draw your sword. Safety first at all times.

So enough of the rules for safety, let us practice some drills.

DRILL NUMBER ONE *(From the Ninja of the Kurama Hachi ryu Tradition)*

Assume the position of iai-hiza, the sword slung across the back, from right shoulder blade to left hip.

The hands should be cupped slightly, and resting midway upon the thighs, in the right hand, hold a piece of folded Echizen-no-kami (sword cleaning paper from Echizen) or if this is unavailable a piece of facial tissue.

Throw the piece of paper up into the air in front of you, using the action of the pressure of the left and right hands in the over the shoulder type of draw, draw and simultaneously strike in iai-nuki-style.

Stop the blade on a line with your left eye, so that the point is slightly lower than your shoulder height. This is important. You must study the correct 'hasuji' at all times (blade attack angle). It is important to make this an angle of about fifteen degrees to the vertical.

Also, when you cut at the piece of paper, do not try to "hit" it, by this I mean, do not try to force the attack upon it, make the hit soft, there is a saying that a soft blade cuts deeply, but a hard blade blunts itself.

If you are using a composite alloy blade, the type that has become known as an iai-to, do not contact hard objects with it, it will break, it is not designed to cut a thing. It is enough to know that you can hit a thrown piece of paper.

Drill Number One

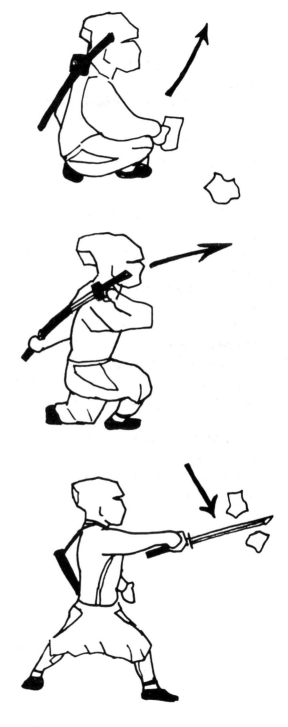

DRILL NUMBER TWO *(From the Amida Brotherhood – Circa 1654)*
This has been passed down in something of a haphazard manner, I include it here as an example of a long redundant form.

Stand with a drawn sword, it is favourable to use Hasso no Kamae (upper engagement position) cut forward stopping the blade at shoulder height, with the arms outstretched. Turning exactly one hundred and eighty degrees cut as your eyes see the target (you must research this well) again stop the blade exactly at shoulder height. This technique has been known as "odan-giri" traversing cut. Next turn to the right ninety degrees executing a cut to the shoulder height, turn one hundred and eighty degrees again in odan-giri style. The rest of the exercise consists of ninety degree movements to change direction followed by odan-giri. The idea is to continue faster and faster, but for the beginning, start off slowly, allowing the cut to come slowly at first, then as the time you are able to do this increases, speed it up, so that you can make many moves and cuts in the space of two minutes. Two minutes at first seems a short time but when you are accomplished at this, you will see that two minutes is in fact a long period of time. As a special "Saikai undo" – purification exercise, the idea is to continue for as much as an hour. Be warned this is spiritually draining, and it should only be attempted if you are of strong and resolute nature. I urge you to be careful, if you feel dizzy or light headed, stop, you are wielding a potentially lethal weapon. Stop and wait for your energy and spirit to return there is no shame in stopping.

121

DRILL NUMBER THREE *(From the Mito Ninja)*

Sometimes known as "Saru-Tobi" — literally "Jumping Monkey", this really is a series of side hops, whilst cutting.

For this, you must make a straight line, this can be either imaginary or a twine string; standing at the end of the line in shizentai hold the sword if your right hand extended out at ninety degrees to the side. With a light step hop to the left side of the line, cutting single-handed to waist height turn and hop to the right side, stabbing out to the suigetsu (Solar plexus) the action is alternate stab-cut —stab cut, though you may experiment with your own variations. Remember it is important to keep either side of the line, make this hopping movement definite. I have heard that there is a similar exercise using the yari spear, which was the favourite technique of the warrior monks of Mount Hiei, if this is the case, then there may be a Chinese origin to the drill of "monkey hopping".

Drill Number Three

This is enough drilling to be going on with. It is always a mistake to be too pedantic, particularly where such a self-expressive art as that of the sword is concerned. I would be most pleased if having studied this book, you are able to evolve your own techniques, referring to free movement.

The following has traditionally been termed "Secret Ways", I must stress, that none of the information that I have gathered in this final section, are the secrets of any martial ryu, that has not allowed them to be divulged; I further want to state, that as regarding the so-called secret ways, it must be noted that such disciplines were the result of battle-proven methods. It is vital to understand it in this context, some of the "secrets" have been left in the original form, due to the fact that at the time of writing, insufficient supportive material has been obtained.

"SECRET WAYS"

In the way of the Sword, there is no opponent.

Seek the path of the Mountain Echo.

Understand that darkness and light are but the same.

Low and high are only matters of opinion.

Seek out the silence at the end of the true cut.

Willow sword meeting bamboo heart.

Victims only are victims.

Life and death are the same.

Truth is a matter of opinion.

Cutting falling blossom

The slow sword pierces deeply, but the harsh sword destroys itself.

A devil mask is only made of clay, strike deeply.

Approach an enemy with your shadow in front of you.

If your opponent is of Itto-Ryu, adopt an Itto-Ryu stance, but cut in Kashima style, this is the way to succeed.

Never let the enemy know the length of your sword.

Make the auspicious signs work for you in combat.

Throw confusion in the face of your enemy, by making him doubt his own skill; this must be accomplished swiftly.

Secret ways

In concluding, it must be said that the skills of the Ninja, whether he was a part of a classical ryu; or a part of a Ninja clan, were the skills of silence and stealth. Silent Kenjutsu was and is the reality of the Ninja heart. Like the heart it must be controlled, otherwise grave crimes can occur.

It is the practice of this supreme method that makes us realise what a link we have with the feudal past. Let us not allow these methods to pass away.

Fencing practice

The past is our heritage,
The present is but the future generations past,
let us make them proud of our efforts to preserve
these skills of our warrior past.

So the time has come again to finish, I stand back from my writing table, and hope that I have done it justice; only you can judge that.

I remain yours sincerely

Katsumi Toda

BIBLIOGRAPHY

For those of you who have requested further details of reference works I add this list to that already contained in the rear of the companion volume "The Ninja Star – Art of Shuriken Jutsu". I trust that this will aid you in your future studies.

JAPANESE WORKS

MINO-TO TAIKAN by Tokuno *(All the major Mino Smiths)*
TO-KEN MORAN by Imura *(Sword Survey)*
BUNGO-TO by Yamada *(Swords made in Bungo Province)*
MIE KEN NO TOKO by Yagase *(Smiths of Ise and Iga)*
ZUKAN TOSO NO SUBETE by Kokubo *(Mountings from the earliest times)*
HIZEN NO KATANA TO TSUBA by Fukunaga and Terada *(Swords and Tsuba made in Hizen Province)*
TANTO by Suzuki *(Tanto from all periods – English index)*
NIPPON-TO SHOKUNIN SHOKUDAN *(Conversations with Swordsmiths etc)*
NIPPON-TO NO SOE KOKATANA by Suenaga *(Companion Blades – Kodzuka)*
KATCHU TO TOKEN by Sato & Ozaki *(Juyo Bunkazai – National Treasures)*
SUISHINSHI MASAHIDE TO SONO ICHIMON by Kuroe *(Life and Work of Masahide)*
TOKO TAIKAN by Tokuno *(Listing of Swordsmiths)*
ECHIZEN NO KAMI SUKEHIRE TAIKAN by Iida *(The family of Sukehiro)*
NIHON TO NO GIMEI by Inuzuka & Fukunaga *(Index of False signatures)*
INOUE SHINKAI TAIKAN by Nakajima & Iida *(the family of Kunisada – "Shinkai")*

NIHON NO BIJUTSU SERIES
    No 24 – Armour
    No 64 – Sword Fittings
    No 73 – Bizen Blades
    No 142 – Masamune & Soshu-Den
SHIN NIHON-TO NO KANTEI NYUMON by Iida & Hiroi *(Sword judgement)*
SHIN SHINTO TAIKAN by Iimura *(including Gendai-To)*
KAJIHEI OSHIGATA *(Tang rubbings of Kajihei Naomitsu, the famous faker)*
JU-KEN by Shibata *(Koto blades)*
SHINTO-SHU by Shibata *(Shinto blades)*
TOSO KINKO JITEN by Wakayama *(Sword furniture metalworkers dictionary)*
NIPPON TOSOGU SHUSEI by Ogasawara *(Catalogue of the Halberstadt collection of sword fittings in Copenhagen) (English part text)*
KATCHU-SHI MEIKAN by Sasama *(Armour makers Signatures)*

BOOKS WITH ENGLISH TEXT

JAPANESE SWORDSMITHS – REVISED by W. M. Hawley *(Over 30,000 listings)*
THE JAPANESE SWORD by Sato *(General reference)*
JAPANESE SWORDS by Ogasawara *(Small reference work)*
EARLY JAPANESE SWORD GUARDS by Sasano *(Sukashi Tsuba)*
JAPANESE ART AND HANDICRAFT by Joly & Tomita *(The famous Red Cross Exhibition of 1916)*

Nunchaku Dynamic Training
BY HIROKAZU KANAZAWA 8TH DAN

Former three time All Japan Karate Champion, and supreme master of the Shotokan style of karate, the author is also a recognised weapons expert, specialising in nunchaku and sai. His book has been acclaimed as the best produced, and easiest to understand on the subject, and takes the reader right from the most basic movements, up to a complex and dynamic 106 move kata, that develops technique and style, as well as providing a dazzling exhibition of skill for demonstration purposes. An in depth work that includes sections on history, origins, author's biography, health aspects etc. 160 pages (9″ x 6″) laminated full colour cover. **$9.95**

Shotokan Advanced Kata Series
BY KEINOSUKE ENOEDA 8TH DAN

Nicknamed the "Shotokan Tiger" by the students and instructors of the prestigious JKA Instructors Institute, this explosive and powerful teacher, who is noted for his practical fighting ability, must surely be the best possible person to present this important series of books. A perfectionist in all he does, the author shows by means of individually hand printed and prepared photographs, and detailed captions, every single movement of these intricate exercises with a degree of clarity never before achieved. A series that should find its way into the collection of every martial artist.

Vol 1 Bassai Dai:Kanku Dai:Jion:Empi:Hangetsu
8″ x 12″ 140 pages **£14.95**
Vol 2 Bassai Sho:Bassai Dai:Jiin:Gankaku:Sochin
8″ x 12″ 111 pages **£14.95**
Vol 3 Tekki-Nidan:Tekki-Sandan (2 versions):Nijushiho:
Gojushiho-Dai:Gojushiho-Sho
8″ x 12″ 111 pages **£14.95**

Shadow of the Ninja
BY KATSUMI TODA

The extensive martial arts and historical knowledge of the author, gives an authenticity and depth to this stirring tale of the Samurai Kuroda and the Ninja of the Tomokatsu clan, that will hold the reader spellbound throughout this beautifully produced book. A fast moving tale of treachery, sudden death and martial excellence in 17th century Japan, made all the more fascinating by original illustrations of Ninja weaponry and techniques. Nine sell-out editions in 25 months proves our claim that "Shadow of the Ninja" sets a new standard for books of this type in quality of production, design and content. 8″ x 5″ 127 pages **$7.95**

Revenge of the Shogun's Ninja
BY KATSUMI TODA

In this sequel to the best selling novel "Shadow of the Ninja" the feud between the Tomokatsu Ninja Clan and the Kuroda Samurai family, moves on a generation as it approaches its dramatic and bloodthirsty conclusion. The secrets of the Ninja are pitted against the supernatural powers of the masters of the spirit of the wind, as the Tomokatsu clan seek out the ghostly green warriors of the forests of Kyushu, for a final dramatic confrontation. An action packed story, full of accurate and intriguing information and lavishly illustrated with line drawings of Ninja techniques and equipment. 8″ x 5″ 107 pages **$7.95**

Ninja Death Vow
BY KATSUMI TODA

As sales of "Shadow of the Ninja" and "Revenge of the Shogun's Ninja" continue to soar, martial arts historian Katsumi Toda, presents the third part of the saga of the Tomokatsu Ninja and their enemies, the Kuroda Samurai. Set against the background of the U.S. Navy's incursion into Japanese waters just over a century ago to break down the barriers of isolation that had existed since 1600, it is a fast moving tale of revenge and treachery. When the Americans threaten to return at a later date and complete their mission, forces who wish to maintain the old system, let loose the power of Ninjutsu to aid their cause, and death and destruction stalk the land. Toda's fast moving style makes the reader feel part of the story; just a page or two into the first chapter, and one can imagine standing on the deck of Commodore Mathew Perry's ship "Mississippi" as the Stars and Stripes fly for the first time over the Japanese waters of Uraga Bay. 144 pages 8½″ x 5½″ **$7.95** (available from November 1985)

The Ninja Star – Art of Shurikenjutsu
BY KATSUMI TODA

Noted Japanese martial arts historian, Katsumi Toda, reveals for the first time the results of his research into the art of star and spike throwing, as practised by the Ninja of medieval Japan. A complete work on this fascinating subject, the book includes; historical background, the development of Ninjutsu, types of shuriken and shaken, stances and grips, throwing techniques, targets, breathing exercises, kata and much more. Lavishly illustrated with attractive line drawings, it is a factual historical work, as well as a practical, down to earth "how to do it" book, and will therefore appeal to martial arts enthusiasts of all ages, styles and affiliations. 79 pages 9″ x 6″ full colour laminated cover, more than 110 illustrations. **$6.95**

Kubotan Keychain – Instrument of Attitude Adjustment
BY TAKAYUKI KUBOTA 8TH DAN

Known to millions as a result of his frequent screen and television appearances, Takayuki Kubota, is a karate master and law-enforcement instructor of exceptional ability, who for two decades has coached the LAPD and other agencies at the highest level. His invention of the "Kubotan" a small plastic baton, (later converted to a keychain) for use by female police officers, revolutionised self-defence in the 70's, and the "Kubotan" itself has become recognised with the passage of time, as probably the most effective, legal self defense aid available to the citizen. In this detailed manual, its inventor shows a wide variety of methods for using the "Kubotan" in almost every imaginable situation. Detailed, high definition photographs and easy to understand text, allow the reader to quickly and fully understand the fine detail of how, and to what parts of the body, the Kubotan can be applied, in order to subdue even the unruliest aggressor. Complete with striking points diagrams, grappling and striking techniques as well as a large selection of the very latest "Kubotan" techniques, the book represents the 'state of the art' in this field. Includes an introduction by Hollywood actor James Caan, 9″ x 6″ 104 pages full colour laminated cover **$7.95**

Dynamic Kicking Method
BY MASAFUMI SHIOMITSU 7TH DAN

There have been so many books on the subject of Karate's kicking techniques, that it is difficult to imagine one that would stand out against the background of boring and often repetitive books currently available. Due to a combination of author ability, excellent design and high quality photography, this one not only stands out, it shines! Author Shiomitsu is an absolute master of the karate kick, not just a talented dilettante, the techniques that he demonstrates and teaches are the original techniques of karate, before they were diluted and packaged for the western market place and are therefore, uncompromisingly tough and brutally effective, rather than athletic or as has been happening of late, theatrical. In this detailed text he not only teaches and demonstrates these techniques, but also includes information on how training and teaching techniques have changed as a result of the efforts to 'sanitize' karate in order to make it an acceptable sport, rather than an effective means of self defence, as well as stories of karate masters who made one or other of these deadly techniques their speciality. Within the covers of this book, is a wealth of information that it would take a lifetime of training to discover. Kicks to cause discomfort, pain, serious injury or worse, depending on the circumstances, and the way that they must be practised to be perfected. These techniques, and his performance of them, have earned the author an awesome reputation, as a particularly hard and dangerous fighter. This encyclopedic work can only endorse the reputation he has acquired as a result of his many victories in and out of the arena over the years. 9″ x 6″ 132 pages colour cover **$9.95**

Balisong – Iron Butterfly
BY CACOY "BOY" HERNANDEZ

We must warn the reader that this is not an instructional book in the normal sense of the word. The techniques shown by Balisong expert Cacoy Hernandez, were developed for, and can only be used in violent circumstances; they have no spiritual value whatsoever. Cacoy ("Boy" to his few friends), Hernandez, is a fighter of the old school, rather than one of the 'actors' that currently seem to dominate the martial arts scene. Born into poverty, raised in deprivation and matured against a background of criminality, he was forced to adopt survival methods, which, although shunned by modern urban society, have allowed him to enjoy six decades, and walk away from countless confrontations. Signor Hernandez has one unshakable belief, which can be summed up by the phrase "Never reject a challenge, and never step back." This book combining as it does his Balisong technique, together with accounts of incidents in his life when he has been forced to use it, must without doubt be of interest to all martial artists. 9″ x 6″ full colour cover, 107 pages **$7.95**

Naked Blade – A Manual of Samurai Swordsmanship
BY TOSHISHIRO OBATA 7TH DAN

Long hidden from the gaze of all but a chosen few the ferocious techniques of swordsmanship as taught by the "Rikugun Toyama Gakko" are revealed for the first time in the English language in this comprehensive and well produced book. Author Toshishiro Obata, is an imposing and highly skilled exponent of this sword method of the former Japanese Imperial Army. The art that he demonstrates, was so feared in the West during the last global conflict that a military training manual published at the time was prompted to advise American officers to "Shoot the officers [with swords] first" as a matter of urgency when confronting the enemy for the first time. The strength, resolve and power of the Samurai lives through the techniques that they developed; they can find no finer repository than in the skill of the author and between the pages of this fascinating training manual. 6″ x 9″ 132 pages **$8.95**

Forthcoming Titles

Close Encounters – The Arresting Art of Taiho Jutsu by Takayuki Kubota
Kama – The Art of the Infinite Circle by Toshishiro Obata

Dragon Books are available from branches of B. Dalton Booksellers, Walden Books and all good martial arts and general bookstores. If you have difficulty obtaining any of these titles, please contact the publisher direct. Orders under $10 can be filled for the advertised price plus $1.50. For orders over $10 simply add 10% to the value of your order to cover freight and handling charges. Overseas customers, please contact us for details of export shipping costs.

Dragon Books P.O. Box 6039 Thousand Oaks CA 91359 USA

Phototypeset in the United Kingdom by Concise Graphics Ltd. Hammersmith London